"As editor of *Charisma*, Lee Grady has always cut through the contemporary religious veneer of men and movements in the charismatic world with profound perception and analytical accuracy. He has been a voice of reason in an unreasonable world of pompous preachers, pulsating music and pillaged pocketbooks. *The Holy Spirit Is Not for Sale* is the heart of Lee Grady poured out on paper to ignite a present fire or rekindle an old fire in your own heart, while not asking you to check your mind at the door. It is a must-read for anyone passionate about a genuine, Pentecostal relationship with God."

—**Dr. Ronald W. Carpenter, Sr.**, presiding bishop, International Pentecostal Holiness Church

"I know of no more discerning, prophetic voice speaking with clarity and compassion and backed by such integrity of character as Lee Grady's. Today's Church needs not only to hear but to heed the wisdom of the warnings set forth in the wisdom of this book."

—**Jack Hayford**, chancellor, The King's College & Seminary; founding pastor, The Church On The Way

"This book should be in every believer's library! Grady trumpets a clarion call to the Body of Christ for a return to godly living and biblical ethics. He speaks with boldness and courage to expose abuse, manipulation and charlatan practices operating in churches and ministries today. *The Holy Spirit Is Not for Sale* will cause you to contend for a fresh move of God's Spirit. I highly recommend this powerful and timely book!"

—**Barbara Wentroble**, president, International Breakthrough Ministries; author, *Removing the Veil of Deception*, *Prophetic Intercession*, and *Praying with Authority*

"While calling us to return to our first love, Lee has provided us with a strong reminder that God's grace is not cheap. May God use this to stir the Body of Christ to be all He expects us to be."

—**Dr. Naomi Dowdy**, senior pastor, Trinity Christian Center (Singapore); founder, Naomi Dowdy Ministries

"I could not put this book down. It is compulsive reading. But it is more than that; it is essential reading for every person who professes to be a charismatic Christian, for all those who are anti-charismatic and also for those who are somewhere in between. I thank God for Lee Grady. This book can only do good. I pray it will have wide distribution, change many lives and ministries, and bring great glory and honor to God."

—from the foreword by **R. T. Kendall**, Ph.D., former minister, Westminster Chapel (London); author, *Total Forgiveness*

"J. Lee Grady is fearlessly sounding the alarm. He exposes sins in the Church and reveals the pathway to true repentance and a lifestyle of holiness. It is my prayer that everyone who reads will awaken to righteousness and ask the Holy Spirit to rekindle the fire of love for God within them. Only then will He send the fires of revival and bring healing to our land."

—**Germaine Copeland**, president, Word Ministries, Inc.; author, *Prayers That Avail Much*

"You have heard the cry of this generation for the authentic message and the messenger. You have seen their hunger for a genuine move of God not orchestrated by man or driven by excellence in promotion and marketing. You have seen them turned off by superstar Christianity and makeup-laden prophets-for-profit who scream 'I' more than they preach Jesus. Buckle up! You have picked by a book written by a man whom God has raised for such a time as this. Lee Grady is one of the most genuine and humble proclaimers I have ever met. He carries a powerful and rare anointing. God is using this man around the world to herald a radical shift among Spirit-empowered people. *The Holy Spirit Is Not for Sale* will rock your world."

—**Sujo John**, laborer for Jesus at Sujo John Ministries; www.sujojohn.com

"In his book *The Holy Spirit Is Not for Sale*, Lee Grady provides a voice for sanity and conscience in the exploding and sometimes turbulent world of Pentecostal and charismatic renewal. I recommend it."

—**Vinson Synan**, Ph.D., dean emeritus, School of Divinity, Regent University

"Although some may find Lee's writing a bit harsh and condemning, if you read carefully, you will hear his heart. It is a heart that loves the Body of Christ and cries out for all of us, himself included, to shake ourselves and be the Church God has called us to be."

—**Joni Lamb**, Daystar Television Network

"*The Holy Spirit Is Not for Sale* stands as a prophetic, clarion call for righteousness and justice under the canopy of Spirit empowerment. This deliberation from Grady, the twenty-first-century American Jeremiah, can serve as the catalyst for a fresh holiness movement established on grace and ignited by God's presence."

—**The Rev. Samuel Rodriguez**, president, National Hispanic Christian Leadership Conference, Hispanic National Association of Evangelicals

"*The Holy Spirit Is Not for Sale* is Lee Grady at his best: powerful, passionate, precise and prophetic. This book should be required reading for every pastor and spiritual leader. With the skill of a surgeon, Grady seeks to expose and cut away the numerous cancers that threaten the very life of the charismatic and Pentecostal movements, refusing to use air freshener to mask the putrid smell of decaying flesh.

"Prophets are never popular. Rather than pander to political correctness, their priority is to please God and not men. Grady's fiery zeal is born, like that of all true prophets, out of a burning desire for God's glory and not man's approval. I believe this book is born of God and has come to the Kingdom for such a time as this. Since those who need this book may well avoid it, do your pastor a favor and buy him a copy. It may save your church and help revive an otherwise dying movement."

—**David Ravenhill**, author and itinerant teacher, Siloam Springs, AR

"Honest, relevant, raw and thought-provoking. Lee is a lion among men who is not afraid to boldly confront the indiscretions in today's Church. Not only does Lee have a pulse on 'Christian' culture, but he is unafraid to touch its nerve. Buckle your seatbelt for the challenge and conviction that ooze from every page!"

—**Jay Lowder,** harvest evangelist; www.jaylowder.com

"What a powerful, convicting book! You must read it. Lee courageously exposes the carnality of American Christians and discloses how crippled the Church has become. May God help us become women and men of integrity, humility and purity.

"Premature responsibility breeds superficiality. In this book, Lee boldly points out that too many of America's pulpits are filled with ministers who are unbroken, power-hungry and who serve at 'the altar of self.' They turn a blind eye to the needs of a lost and dying world to engage in 'Hollywood-style religion,' which too often includes perversion, adultery, greed and lies.

"Tears are flowing down my face as I write this endorsement. I hunger for Jesus every day of my life and long to help facilitate a worldwide awakening! This is also the plea of Lee's book. O Jesus, help us! Reader, don't you dare miss reading Lee's timely book."

—**Alice Smith,** executive director, U.S. Prayer Center
(Houston, TX); www.EddieandAlice.com

"J. Lee Grady did not author *The Holy Spirit Is Not for Sale* for accolades, royalties or controversy. Born out of a burden for Pentecostals and charismatics who have lost their way, this book was written to call them back to Spirit-empowerment."

—**Hal Donaldson,** president, Convoy of Hope

THE
HOLY SPIRIT
IS NOT
FOR SALE

THE HOLY SPIRIT IS NOT FOR SALE

Rekindling the Power of God
in an Age of Compromise

J. LEE GRADY

Chosen

a division of Baker Publishing Group
Grand Rapids, Michigan

© 2010 by J. Lee Grady

Published by Chosen Books
a division of Baker Publishing Group
P.O. Box 6287, Grand Rapids, MI 49516–6287
www.chosenbooks.com

Based on *What Happened to the Fire*, published in 1994

Printed in the United States of America

Library of Congress Cataloging-in-Publication Data

Grady, J. Lee.
    The Holy Spirit is not for sale: rekindling the power of God in an age of compromise / J. Lee Grady.
      p.   cm.
    Includes bibliographical references.
    ISBN 978-0-8007-9487-3 (pbk.)
    1. Pentecostalism. I. Title.
    BR1644.G725 2010
    270.8′2—dc22

2009047093

10 11 12 13 14 15 16   7 6 5 4 3 2 1

This book is dedicated to the young Christian leaders I have had the honor of mentoring and encouraging in recent years: Agus, A.J., Aleksandr, Bálint, Billy, Brandon, Charles, Chris, David, Doug, Felipe, Gennady, Gideon, Jackson, Jason, Jeet, Jojo, Jonathan, Jusan, Louis, Luís, Lyndle, Lyrica, Marvin, Mike, Miracle, Moses, Nicole, Quentin, Raja, Rick, Robert, Sabin, Shibu, Steve, Sven, Swanky, Yinka and Xavier.

Contents

Foreword by R. T. Kendall 13
Preface 17
Introduction: Rekindling the Fire 25

1 Hot Coals from Heaven's Altar 37
2 The Fire of Supernatural Anointing 51
3 The Fire of Boldness 69
4 The Fire of Purity 81
5 The Fire of Integrity 99
6 The Fire of Humility 113
7 The Fire of Truth 131
8 The Fire of Justice 149
9 The Fire of Spiritual Liberty 167
10 The Fire of Prayer 181
11 The Fire of Genuine Love 199
12 How to Have Your Own Personal Pentecost 211

How to Be Baptized in the Holy Spirit 223
Notes 227
Index 231

Foreword

I could not put this book down. It is compulsive reading. But it is more than that; it is essential reading for every person who professes to be a charismatic Christian, for all those who are anti-charismatic and also for those who are somewhere in between.

I never expected to see a book like this, especially coming from the pen of the bold editor of *Charisma* magazine. If you found yourself reading this amazing book and did not know who the author of it was, you would have thought it was written by a theological cessationist, a five-point Calvinist or an anti-charismatic evangelical who couldn't wait to expose the likes and the lies of some of those household name TV evangelists many see all the time. But no. It is written by Lee Grady, a charismatic himself, who thunders like an Old Testament prophet on every page—taking up the cause of the persecuted Church, calling for sound teaching, preaching Pentecost and warning all of us of fraudulent, flamboyant and greedy preachers—*calling a good number of them by name*—who have deceived innocent people all over the globe, right, left and center.

And yet a book like this is long overdue. I just pray it will do some good. What good? Two things. First, that there will be an open, unfeigned repentance coming from the hearts of those leaders who have been right in the middle of all the sham Lee exposes. This book—just maybe—could do it. It might well be used of the Holy Spirit to awaken key charismatic leaders who up to now have dug in their heels rather than admit to being imprudent about certain preachers and certain alleged moves of the Holy Spirit. It would show great humility were these leaders to say they got it wrong. Who knows but that God would honor such vulnerability by granting a greater blessing of the Holy Spirit than ever? It would show, too, that such leaders are true men of God after all.

Second, this book—just maybe—could awaken many of those sincere Christians who have ardently followed these preachers by sending in their money and using their credit cards in order to receive personal financial blessing. Such people, though utterly sincere, are encouraged to give out of greediness more than love for God. Lee tells us to beware of every church leader whose message seems to be money-centered. That covers more charismatic preachers than one cares to think about. Lee reckons that those leaders who claim to have a "debt-breaking anointing"—the promise that God will get you out of debt if you send these leaders your money—should not be trusted. But those who trusted them could be touched by this book by ceasing to support such ministers for personal financial help.

I have wished for a long time that God would raise up a Martin Luther among the charismatic movement who would do in our day what Luther did in his. Luther exposed the wickedness of leaders who led innocent people to buy indulgences to get them out of purgatory. Lee Grady demonstrates similar courage; he wonders whatever is the difference between medieval Christians buying indulgences and present-day Christians sending their money to preachers for personal gain. I am in awe of the author's boldness and clarity but thrilled with his honesty and integrity.

This book should drive us to our knees. Lee contrasts Christianity between the First World and the Third World, focusing especially on China, where Christians *expect* persecution, not money; where they pursue God without miracles being their goal, and yet *see* real miracles, including the dead being raised! It should bring us to deep repentance, personal holiness and a genuine fear of God. The absence of the fear of God is at the bottom of so much sexual promiscuity and financial extravagance, which Lee writes openly about. The issue of character versus gift emerges in bold relief. It is a stunning hitting-the-bull's-eye rebuke to those who believe that their anointing surpasses character. Lee calls for all of us to be transparently accountable, having no secrets, to embrace sexual purity and to maintain financial integrity in all uses of money.

The *Charisma* editor also issues a plea for sound teaching. It could be argued that the lack of solid teaching is what created the vacuum filled by superficial ministry. Lee quotes Charles Spurgeon, "The most fervid revivalism will wear itself out in mere smoke if it is not maintained by the fuel of teaching. Sound teaching is the best protection for heresies that ravage right and left among us."

This book could be a turning point for the charismatic movement, both in the way many in it see themselves and also in the way they are perceived by others. It could even cause some evangelicals to lower their voices regarding what they have said so critically about charismatics, and respect charismatics when they see a man like Lee Grady in his position saying what he says in this book.

I thank God for Lee Grady. This book can only do good. I pray it will have wide distribution, change many lives and ministries and bring great glory and honor to God.

—R. T. Kendall

For this reason I remind you to kindle afresh the gift of God which is in you through the laying on of my hands.

2 Timothy 1:6

Do not quench the Spirit.

1 Thessalonians 5:19

On the Day of Pentecost, God poured out His Holy Spirit on the waiting, willing disciples. They received, prophesied, and preached everywhere—the Lord working with them, and confirming the Word with signs following. The hour of God's visitation in the last days is upon us. As with the former rain, there must be receptive hearts and willing co-workers with God. We have received as on the Day of Pentecost. We must present our bodies, our lives, and our all on His sacred altar to carry this holy flame to the ends of the world. Pentecost is tailored of God for this very hour. Beloved, it is powerful and altogether sufficient for the need. Let us march under its banner and its cloud of blessing to God's appointed victory.

Ralph M. Riggs, Superintendent of the Assemblies of God, 1953–1959[1]

Preface

Cuban pastor Emilio Gonzales had never heard of the term *baptism in the Holy Spirit* until one Sunday in the mid-1950s. That was when a Methodist bishop from Mexico visited the Vedado Methodist Church in downtown Havana. The old bishop asked everyone in the congregation to kneel and pray for God's Spirit to empower them, and Emilio, who was just entering the ministry at the time, followed his instructions eagerly.

What followed was Emilio's personal version of Pentecost. He described his experience to me in the fall of 1993, when I visited Havana to investigate how churches had been faring since Fidel Castro relaxed restrictions on religion in Cuba.

A frail man with a gentle smile, Emilio told me in vivid detail about his first encounter with the Baptizer.

"I began to feel an electric current go from my head to my feet," he said. "I lifted my hands and began crying and laughing. I felt I had been bathed in God's presence."

After this unusual event, the Mexican bishop left town. Emilio had no one with whom to compare his experience and no access to books about the Holy Spirit. All he had was his Bible.

"I had to judge for myself," he told me. "I examined everything very carefully. No one else understood it."

Though it seemed like an insignificant moment, what happened that day at the Vedado Methodist Church would dramatically change Cuba's spiritual climate. A fire was ignited that would spread quietly throughout the island—a fire that would prove to be unquenchable, even in a country in which Christian belief was discouraged and pastors were routinely banished to prison camps.

In the years following Cuba's 1959 Marxist revolution, many of the Methodist pastors who didn't flee their homeland were "strangely warmed" by the same fire that burned in Emilio's heart. Rinaldo Hernandez, then a young seminarian studying at a Methodist school in the city of Matanzas, discovered the heaven-sent fire in 1979 when a visiting professor from the United States told students at a chapel service that she had been baptized in the Holy Spirit. Rinaldo, his wife and some other students prayed for an infilling of God's power and began speaking in tongues.

A few months later, before he could finish his studies, Rinaldo was labeled a criminal by the Cuban government and sent to a labor camp. But the fire he encountered at the seminary in Matanzas only burned more brightly during those dark days he spent away from his wife and infant daughter. The Holy Spirit's presence renewed and invigorated him, and confirmed to him that God had called him to share Christ with his countrymen.

When I met Rinaldo in 1993, he was pastoring a lively congregation of young people—many of them new converts—at the same Vedado church where Emilio Gonzales had been baptized in the Spirit forty years earlier. The Communists were not interfering with the work of the church, and the young people worshiped without fear of recrimination.

"We are not praying for a revival," Rinaldo told me. "We are *in* a revival. There is a growing church in Cuba, a powerful and dynamic church. This movement is quiet, but strong."

Like the majority of Methodist churches in Cuba, Rinaldo's congregation is fully charismatic in doctrine and worship style. On a typical Wednesday night at the Vedado Methodist Church, the young members clap, shake tambourines and raise their hands as they sing lively praise choruses. Some of them stood in front of the congregation and shared words of prophecy and exhortation.

Just east of Havana in Marianao, Emilio Gonzales was pastoring a large Methodist church, with the same charismatic format. It was in full evidence when I stopped in for a visit.

Charismatic renewal has transformed an entire denomination in Cuba—a denomination not known for the same kind of evangelical fervor in the United States. According to Rinaldo, an estimated 75 percent of Methodist pastors in his country consider themselves charismatic or Pentecostal. It is possible that the entire Methodist denomination in Cuba could be experiencing renewal within a few years.

How did this happen? As renewal fires spread during the 1970s and 1980s, churches began to evangelize in spite of government intimidation. After Castro aired a landmark apology in 1990 for discriminating against Christians, the Methodists started one hundred new churches within three years. Other Pentecostal groups, such as the Assemblies of God and the Pentecostal Holiness Church, were also growing at impressive rates, as more and more Cubans realized they were free to believe.

One night during my visit to Cuba, I drove with Rinaldo to observe what he called a house church located in the Havana suburb of Cojimar. As we drove past crumbling buildings and austere Communist monuments, I imagined that the meeting would take place in a tiny living room with a dozen people. When we arrived, I was surprised to find 125 believers of all ages jammed into the front yard of a modest concrete block home. The worshipers, all of whom had walked or ridden bicycles to get to the church service, were singing when we

arrived. Their praises could be heard all over the neighborhood, but no one seemed to mind.

As I took my seat on a cold stone step and began to clap
along, I was struck by how joyful these Cuban believers were.
Their voices were exuberant, their eyes glowed with radiance
and their bright smiles made up for a power shortage that had
forced them to meet in total darkness—except for a single
kerosene lantern hanging on a wire by the front porch.

As we began to sing a reverent worship song in Spanish,
most people closed their eyes and lifted their hands toward
heaven. A few shed tears as they praised God for His love and
mercy. But I could not close my eyes. I was too busy gazing
at the remarkable scene.

How can these people be so happy? I thought. I knew the
kinds of conditions they lived in. I knew they had eaten very
little that day, except for maybe some rice or bread. I knew
that life in Cuba was marked by hardship and pain. Yet these
Christians seemed to be living in a realm of faith that was as
foreign to me as their language and customs.

After we finished singing, several people stood to give
testimonies about how God had helped them walk through
the trials of the week. One young woman said she had been
converted because some women from the church visited her in
the hospital and prayed for her healing. God delivered her of
cancer, she said, adding that she went home and destroyed her
Santeria idols and other occult fetishes. Later, in his lengthy
sermon, Rinaldo used the woman's story to illustrate that
God wants to perform miracles today just as He did during
Jesus' earthly ministry.

When we closed the service with more singing, I studied
the scene again in amazement, tears filling my eyes. Never in
my life had I witnessed a more genuine expression of Christianity. *This must be what the New Testament church was
like,* I thought.

When I returned to my hotel room, from which I could
look out over the city of Havana, I pondered what God had

been doing on that isolated island over the past forty years. In spite of scarcity, Marxist control, officially sanctioned atheism and total isolation from the United States, the fire of God's Spirit had been sweeping the country. The blaze of spiritual renewal that began in the 1950s had proven more powerful than Castro's regime. I knew it would outlive Marxism in Cuba.

Before I left Havana, I sat down with Rinaldo Hernandez and the bishop of the Methodist Church of Cuba, Joel Ajo. We talked about the revival and about the needs of the churches there: training for ministers, youth ministry materials, Sunday school literature and, most of all, simple encouragement. Eager to take advantage of new opportunities to minister in Cuba, the bishop extended a warm invitation to American church groups to visit his country.

Suddenly I was disturbed. I wanted American Christians to see for themselves how the Spirit was transforming the churches of Cuba, yet it pained me to think we might infect Cuban congregations with the same disease that has quenched and snuffed out the fires of revival in our own country.

These Cuban church leaders have more to offer us in the United States, it seemed to me, *than we can possibly offer them. Perhaps it would be better for Cuban pastors to come to America*, I thought, *and teach us what the Holy Spirit has taught them.*

I breathed a prayer of desperation as I imagined a worst-case scenario: *Lord, don't let us charismatics bring our money-centered gospel to these starving people. Don't let us mislead these precious saints with our own misguided doctrines. And most of all, Lord, don't let us duplicate our denominational divisions here in a place where every believer needs the support of the entire Body of Christ.*

As I boarded my plane at José Martí Airport in Havana and returned to Miami, I thought much about the state of the churches in my country. I was haunted by one question: What happened to the fire in America's churches? Thousands of pastors in America have been "strangely warmed" by the same Holy Spirit who impacted men like Emilio Gonzales and Rinaldo Hernandez. Hundreds of thousands of charismatic churches have been started in the United States since the early 1970s. Yet church growth has stagnated in recent years. In most American churches, the fire of Pentecost is no longer blazing.

If Cuba's churches were languishing today, their leaders could easily blame their condition on a lack of resources. It has only been since 1990, after all, that Bibles became available there in government-run stores. But the spiritual coldness that exists in American churches cannot be blamed on a lack of resources. We publish more Bibles, hymnals, Christian books and church literature than any nation on earth, and we use most of what we publish within our own borders. We spend millions of dollars on church buildings and denominational facilities. We have conferences on every imaginable topic, and we offer programs designed to cure every spiritual problem. But our churches are not on fire for God.

Why does spiritual revival seem so elusive to us?

I have pondered that question for several years, since I was once part of a revival movement that collapsed because of human weaknesses. Although I believe that God sovereignly gives revival, I also believe that revival cannot occur unless God's people are committed to following not their own agenda but the agenda of the Holy Spirit. Too many times in this century, movements that were born of the Spirit ended up as spiritual miscarriages. And in every case, men and women were responsible for derailing God's holy purpose.

The thesis of this book is simple: Charismatic churches in America today are laden down with tons of baggage that needs to be thrown overboard. If we would reject our misguided mysticism, our smug elitism and our hollow egotism, I believe our churches would be aflame with holy zeal. If we would renounce our bizarre infatuation with money and success, I believe, God would grant us true passion for the

Savior. If we would stop mistreating the flock of God, He might give us many more sheep to tend. And, most importantly, if we would stop building our own human-centered kingdoms, He might afford us the honor of playing a part in building His.

I am not a theologian or pastor, so I do not offer in this book an exhaustive scriptural thesis on how we can secure spiritual renewal in this country. But I have made it my business as a journalist to observe the charismatic renewal movement—a movement of which I am part. This book is my admittedly feeble but honest attempt to identify some of the reasons our fire is not burning brightly like the fire I witnessed in Cuba—a fire that is also blazing in many other parts of the world today.

Some two millennia ago the apostle Paul urged the Christians of Thessalonica to keep their fire white-hot. "Do not quench the Spirit," he told them (1 Thessalonians 5:19, RSV). The Living Bible translation says, "Do not smother the Holy Spirit."

Yet since the first century men have frustrated the work of the Spirit with their own carnality. In this book, I point out ten specific things that have smothered the Spirit in charismatic and Pentecostal churches in America, including mysticism, elitism, separatism, authoritarianism, egotism and greed.

My simple prayer is that God would purge us of all these things, so that the Spirit can have His way. May God ignite a new fire in our midst and grant us a new Pentecost.

But if I say, "I will not remember Him or speak anymore in His name," then in my heart it becomes like a burning fire shut up in my bones; and I am weary of holding it in, and I cannot endure it.

Jeremiah 20:9

Above all, feed the flame with intimate fellowship with Christ. No man was ever cold in heart who lived with Jesus on such terms as John and Mary did of old, for He makes men's hearts burn within them. I never met a half-hearted preacher who was much in communion with the Lord Jesus. The zeal of God's house ate up our Lord, and when we come into contact with Him it begins to consume us also.

Charles Spurgeon, *Lectures to My Students*

Introduction

Rekindling the Fire

Unless you are Rip Van Winkle and have been asleep for years, I'm sure you feel the daily convulsions that are rocking our world. Change is hitting America squarely between the eyes. Everything that can be shaken is being shaken—from banks and insurance companies to car manufacturers and media empires.

Trusted brands are going out of business. Home values have plunged. Newspapers are laying off employees in droves as readers go digital; bookstores can't compete with online retailers. Pontiac is officially dead, and the city of Detroit—once the proud global headquarters of the auto industry—is rusting. And the Christian publishing industry is in shambles as we face what journalists have called "the media recession."

What the world is experiencing today is more than an economic tsunami. The upheaval is affecting us politically, socially, technologically and spiritually. It feels as if God has pushed a giant red reset button in heaven. Change is being forced on us, and we are not handling it well.

Meanwhile there is a similar problem in the Church: We Christians don't have a great track record when it comes to embracing change. We are slow adapters. Often we insist on doing church like Grandpa did, and when we realize we're outdated it's too late.

I've been pondering the changes happening in charismatic churches particularly and praying about our future as a movement. I've been asking hard questions and wrestling with my own fears of change. And I've reached an uncomfortable conclusion, namely that the charismatic movement as we know it has ended.

There. I've said it. Some will hate me for it. But it seems obvious to me that God has moved on.

I celebrate what God did to bring the Holy Spirit's renewal to the church in recent years. My life was totally changed by it. But the cloud of His presence is moving, and we cannot pitch our tents around past revivals. While we embrace the eternal things He gave us in those days, we must discard styles and methods that are no longer fruitful so we can advance.

That doesn't mean we throw the baby out with the bathwater. We cling to what is good (1 Thessalonians 5:21). But what began as a dynamic explosion of the Holy Spirit's life and power has become increasingly shallow. The tide has gone out, leaving on the shore all kinds of debris.

We love what God did for us in previous revivals. But we must leave behind the excesses, extremes and flaky doctrines that give charismatics a bad name. The day of the one-man show is over. The prosperity circus was a failure. We must abandon the deceptive hype of the past. People today are craving authenticity—not hollow words and empty promises.

I believe a new-generation church is emerging. I visit two or three churches every month in this country. Although they still preach the core charismatic doctrines of the infilling of the Holy Spirit, those that are healthy and growing have developed new paradigms. Though they embrace the Holy Spirit's *charisms*, or spiritual gifts, they also place high value on evangelism, small-group discipleship, social justice and world missions.

They are extravagant in giving to outreach. They are relational, not event-driven. And they demand character from leaders rather than simply celebrating a man or woman's spiritual anointing. They also have made a proactive effort to distance themselves from the "dark side" of the charismatic movement—by rejecting pride, carnality, money-focused messages and unbridled mysticism.

No one has coined a term for this new movement yet, but it is growing—and it represents the future of charismatic Christianity in our country. These new-generation churches embrace healthy leadership and don't tolerate the kind of ministry monkey business that has embarrassed us in recent years. These churches love sinners and preach grace, but they draw the lines necessary to enforce biblical standards.

I've come to know many of the pastors and leaders of this new movement in recent years. They sense a new wind of spiritual renewal blowing across the land, even at a time when secularism is encroaching.

New-generation churches are also connected in a healthy, relational way to other churches, and they are not denominational in a restrictive sense. They refuse labels. Rather than wearing the cumbersome armor of a religious structure, their leaders are free to pray, dream and be creative about how they should reach children, high school students, business leaders, drug addicts, immigrants, homeless people, twentysomethings and church dropouts in their communities.

These churches also believe that God is tearing down the walls that divide us within the faith. For too long we've been content to congregate in our comfortable tribal groups. But the essence of Pentecost involves the Holy Spirit's outpouring "on all mankind" (Acts 2:17). This means true Pentecostals cannot harbor racism.

God's agenda in this next season of revival will involve tearing down racist structures—and this will occur not only in white churches but in black and Hispanic ones as well. It also means that church leaders from China, India, the Middle East, Africa and Latin America will have a greater platform to speak into our lives here in the United States. Western Christians must accept the fact that we don't have all the answers!

New-generation churches also know that we face an unprecedented global opportunity for evangelism. They embrace technological progress without putting their trust in it. They have claimed all new media—from iPhones to BlackBerries to Twitter and Facebook—so every person on this planet can hear that Jesus died to save us.

I've never been the first to try new gadgets. I still like to hold my newspaper and read it on the back porch—and I don't (yet) watch TV shows on my telephone. But regardless of my creature habits, I can't stand in the way of today's technological revolution. I recognize that I must change when God pushes the reset button. Rather than holding onto the security of the past, I've decided to get out of the boat and follow Jesus into uncharted territory. I think we all need to.

Leaving Dead Things Behind

Some people might be offended when they hear me say the charismatic movement is dead. After I wrote this in *Charisma* magazine in 2009, one woman accused me of heresy, because—in her words—I believe "the age of the Holy Spirit has ended." I didn't say that. But I think we need to be honest as we face the condition of our movement, a condition I seek to lay out in this book.

I am not a coroner. But the historic period we call the American charismatic movement ended a while ago. By making that pronouncement I am not saying that (1) the Holy Spirit isn't moving today, (2) the miraculous gifts of the Holy

Spirit aren't available to us any more or (3) people who are associated with this movement are all washed up.

On the contrary, we could be on the cusp of one of the most dynamic spiritual awakenings in history, and it will most certainly be accompanied by the supernatural work of God's Spirit. Yet if we want to shift with Him into the next season we must lay aside old mindsets and worn-out religious paradigms that we picked up during the past forty years.

The history books will record that the charismatic movement began in 1967 with the Duquesne revival among Roman Catholics in Pittsburgh (there were earlier birth pangs with Episcopalians and Presbyterians in the late 1950s and early 1960s) and that the movement waned by the late 1980s. Charismatic renewal was a visitation of God—ushering millions of people from mainline church backgrounds into an experience with the Holy Spirit and renewing many older Pentecostal churches.

There were subsequent outpourings of the Holy Spirit in the 1990s, of course—namely the Toronto Blessing of 1994 and the Pensacola Revival the following year—but the overall movement was fragmenting. The televangelism scandals of 1987 and the implosion of what was known as the Discipleship Movement two years later made it obvious that something was rotten underneath the polished veneer of charismania. By that time, many of the mainline Protestants who had been impacted by this movement had become disaffected, and many Catholics had returned to their parishes and left the renewal behind.

This is not to say that the renewal movement didn't impact the worldwide Church on a grand scale. It certainly did—especially when Christians who were touched by the Spirit's power launched ministries in the United States and abroad. Huge advances have occurred on the international mission field as the result of Spirit-empowered charismatics who actually did something with the anointing they received during that season.

Yet we must also admit that some of the most notable spiritual trends occurring in the United States in recent years have been associated with evangelicals who don't have ties to charismatics. These include Rick Warren, Beth Moore, Louie Giglio, Henry Blackaby, Bill Hybels, Andy Stanley and Erwin McManus. We are naïve (and arrogant) if we think the only people God is using in this hour are members of our own charismatic subculture.

When I say the charismatic movement is dead I am issuing a challenge. It is time for us to lay aside the past so we can embrace the future. We are in a season when church leaders should be asking the hard questions:

- Are we locked into the past in an unhealthy way?
- Are we using language, methods or ministry styles that are stale, dated and ineffective?
- Are we training younger people to lead the next generation?
- Are we willing to slaughter any sacred cows and pet doctrines that hinder outreach and church growth?

Old Testament laws forbade people from touching anything dead (Leviticus 21:1, 11). That's because corpses spread disease. Dead things stink and defile. This is certainly true of dead religion. It can make a church barren and lifeless, even if it is hidden under a superficial coating of trendy songs and informal dress. It's not enough to update your music and take off your tie. We need the new life of the Spirit. Something new must happen inside us.

God once told Moses to put a bronze serpent on a stick and hold it in the air. When people looked at the snake they were healed. Centuries later, King Hezekiah destroyed this image because people had begun to worship it (2 Kings 18:4). What God meant for good later became a hindrance. Sometimes spiritual things have an expiration date!

Of course God's moral law never changes, and neither does His character. But He may not move today in the same way He did in 1975; the strategies He gave us in 1990 are not necessarily useful to churches now. The Holy Spirit doesn't want us to follow a rote formula; He wants us to seek His presence as He moves through history.

It really doesn't matter what we label this next movement. What's important is His renewing presence. Rather than worshiping God around a monument to the past, we must find out where He's going and follow the glory cloud.

A Strong Wind Advisory

The book of Acts begins and ends with intriguing references to wind. We are well acquainted with Luke's description of the wind mentioned in Acts 2:

> When the day of Pentecost came, they were all together in one place. Suddenly a sound like the blowing of a violent wind came from heaven and filled the whole house where they were sitting. They saw what seemed to be tongues of fire that separated and came to rest on each of them. All of them were filled with the Holy Spirit and began to speak in other tongues as the Spirit enabled them. . . .
>
> Then Peter stood up with the Eleven, raised his voice and addressed the crowd: "Fellow Jews and all of you who live in Jerusalem, let me explain this to you. . . . This is what was spoken by the prophet Joel: 'In the last days, God says, I will pour out my Spirit on all people.'"
>
> Acts 2:1–4, 14, 16–17, NIV

The outpouring of the Holy Spirit in the first century, "like the blowing of a violent wind," provided the impetus for a movement that ultimately conquered the Roman world. The Egyptians, Medes, Cretans, Arabs and other foreign visitors to Jerusalem who witnessed the miracle of Pentecost had no reason to believe that the tiny band preaching on the street would soon shake the Empire to its foundations, but that is exactly what took place within three hundred years. Like leaven in a lump of dough, the message of Christ quickly permeated the known world and became the dominant force in all of history.

The Gospel that began as an insignificant mustard seed soon grew, as Jesus had predicted, to become the most massive tree in the garden. The sound of Pentecost's rushing wind, like an awesome typhoon, altered the moral and spiritual terrain of three continents.

Yet the book of Acts closes with a different kind of wind. In chapters 27 and 28 we read of the apostle Paul's journey to Rome as a prisoner under the watchful eye of an imperial centurion. When the centurion declined to heed Paul's warning against changing winter ports, a "wind of hurricane force" (Acts 27:14, NIV) drove the Roman vessel from its planned destination and raged for fourteen days. The storm destroyed the ship and it looked as if the whole crew would drown, but God intervened miraculously, enabling His apostolic messenger ultimately to debark in Rome. There Paul preached the Gospel of Christ in the court of Caesar himself.

It is no coincidence that the book of Acts begins and ends with these references to wind. I believe it is the Holy Spirit's way of signifying to us that we cannot experience the wind of Acts 2 without encountering the raging storm as well. The same Jesus who baptizes in the Holy Spirit also baptizes in fire.

The violent east-northeast wind drove the Roman ship across the Adriatic Sea in the direction of Rome, while the wind of Pentecost flung the seeds of the Gospel to the four corners of the world within a few short years. The fire of the Holy Spirit provided the apostles with supernatural ability to carry out their passionate missionary endeavors. The early Church leaders had little to rely on in the way of human ability: They had no organization or corporate structure, no elaborate communications technology, no proven methods of evangelism or discipleship, no Bible, no seminary training. It was the Holy Spirit who enabled these unlearned men to turn the world upside down.

Since the events of the book of Acts, Christians throughout history have hoped that a heavenly wind might blow in their day. Whenever the Church has experienced a lull in her growth or a dampening of her fervor, spiritual revivals and renewal movements have appeared on the scene, releasing anew the Holy Spirit's power to energize the Church for her worldwide mission. With each fresh revival movement, new ground has been claimed for the Kingdom of God.

The ebb and flow of the history of the Church has been marked by many such revivals down through the centuries. This was certainly the case when the modern Pentecostal movement began in the United States at the beginning of the twentieth century. Although tainted at times by human failure, the movement made a pivotal impact on the Church worldwide that is only beginning to be understood today.

The Pentecostal explosion has not been without its problems. Fast growth often produces mutation. It is difficult to deny that the Pentecostal/charismatic movement has produced good fruit: millions of people converted to Christ, churches planted, spiritual passion ignited. Yet in the short history of the movement, it has also produced its share of wood, hay and stubble.

Those involved in Pentecostalism or the charismatic renewal have experienced the excitement of the wind of Acts 2. We have sensed the Spirit's anointing. Our churches have brought countless numbers of Christians into a deeper, more personal relationship with Christ. Yet at the same time, doctrinal excesses, hyperspirituality, legalism and various unorthodox practices have succeeded at times in discrediting what is valid.

That is why I believe we are about to be visited by another wind—a wind much like the one that battered the Roman ship in Acts 27. It is time for those of us who believe in the gifts of the Holy Spirit for today to pass through the storm and allow what is false to be swept away. Some of the structures we have built over the years will be broken up underneath us in the midst of the tempest, but our message will be refined in the process. God cannot give permanence to the work of our hands unless it has been tested. We must face into the wind.

What Are You Building?

Every state in this country has strict building codes. You can't just buy a piece of land and throw up a structure any way you choose. Local governments have standards for foundations, floors, drywall, roofs, exhaust systems, water heaters, wiring, lighting and sanitary drainage. In my neighborhood you can't even erect a shed in your backyard without a permit, and an inspector will always drop by unannounced to make sure you followed the rules.

In Florida, where I live, these codes are very important. You don't want to discover during a hurricane that your contractor used shoddy plywood or defective concrete when he built your house or condo. Bad construction just might send your roof into a neighbor's yard!

It's ironic that our society doesn't tolerate sloppy building, yet in the charismatic church we place little emphasis on code enforcement. In fact, in our freewheeling movement we celebrate the independent spiritual contractor who uses questionable materials and answers to no one. Much of our movement during the past thirty years has been built like this—and today we are discovering that what we thought was sturdy was actually stuck together with cheap nails, substandard wood, thin glue and duct tape.

I hear a creaking sound—and it is the sagging of rafters. The Lord has entered our crooked house with His holy plumb line and a clipboard—and He is not pleased.

Did you know God has a building code? I prefer the way *The Message* Bible translates the apostle Paul's words in 1 Corinthians 3:12–15: "Take particular care in picking out your building materials. Eventually there is going to be an inspection. If you use cheap or inferior materials, you'll be found out. The inspection will be thorough and rigorous. You won't get by with a thing. If your work passes inspection, fine; if it doesn't, your part of the building will be torn out and started over. But *you* won't be torn out; you'll survive—but just barely."

Paul says Jesus will inspect our buildings using the ultimate test—the fire of His holiness. The New American Standard Bible translation says: "Now if any man builds on the foundation with gold, silver, precious stones, wood, hay, straw, each man's work will become evident...the fire itself will test the quality of each man's work" (verses 12–13). We must prepare for a building inspection. If we ignore God's codes our churches and ministries will not stand in the day of visitation.

Each chapter of this book examines various qualities that we must embrace if we intend to build lives and churches that will survive the test of God. I pray that we are ready for our inspection. As the storm winds blow, may God give us the grace to renovate the areas of our lives, our churches and our ministries that have not been built according to His standards.

There is surely a fresh fire available to us today. The apostle Paul told his spiritual son Timothy to "kindle afresh the gift of God which is in you through the laying on of my hands" (2 Timothy 1:6). Even when old moves of God die out because of carnality, pride, division or religiosity, the Spirit is ever ready to send a fresh Pentecost. May we wrestle with God until He sends that blessing from heaven.

Questions for Discussion

1. How did you come to experience the power of the Holy Spirit for the first time?
2. List some of the positive benefits of the charismatic renewal that you have witnessed, either in your own life or in the lives of others.
3. In what ways do you think charismatic churches need to change in order to become more effective?
4. Can you think of any dead charismatic traditions that you need to put aside?
5. When you consider God's holy building code for His church, what areas of your personal life need reformation?

Then one of the seraphim flew to me with a burning coal in his hand, which he had taken from the altar with tongs. He touched my mouth with it and said, "Behold, this has touched your lips; and your iniquity is taken away and your sin is forgiven." Then I heard the voice of the Lord, saying, "Whom shall I send, and who will go for Us?" Then I said, "Here am I. Send me!"

Isaiah 6:6–8

As for me, I baptize you with water for repentance, but He who is coming after me is mightier than I, and I am not fit to remove His sandals; He will baptize you with the Holy Spirit and fire. His winnowing fork is in His hand, and He will thoroughly clear His threshing floor; and He will gather His wheat into the barn, but He will burn up the chaff with unquenchable fire.

Matthew 3:11–12

It was the Holy Ghost who was given to the church at Pentecost; and it is the Holy Ghost who gives Pentecostal blessings now. It is this power, given to bless men, that wrought such wonderful life, and love, and self-sacrifice in the early church; and it is this that makes us look back to those days as the most beautiful part of the Church's history. And it is the same Spirit of power that must dwell in the hearts of all believers in our day to give the Church its true position. Let us ask God then, that every minister and Christian worker may be endued with the power of the Holy Ghost.

Andrew Murray, South African
pastor and author (1828–1917)[1]

1

Hot Coals from Heaven's Altar

Moriah Chapel in Loughor, Wales, is not a fancy building. Constructed in 1898 and surrounded by crumbling tombstones, the church is plain and uninviting except for a monument near the front door that might be mistaken for a war memorial. It is, in fact, one of the few tributes to Evan Roberts, the young Welshman who preached in the chapel in the fall of 1904 and triggered one of the greatest Christian revivals in modern history.

In the fall of 2008 I stood inside the chapel and studied its plain walls and the rickety stairs leading up to the narrow balcony. I got behind the wooden pulpit and looked over the empty pews, some carved with initials. I stood beside Roberts's modest grave, which was in a small, crowded cemetery behind the chapel. I was reminded that God uses the weak things of the world to confound the wise.

There was nothing outwardly remarkable about Roberts or the place his ministry began. He was the simple son of a coal miner. He worked as a blacksmith yet aspired to be a minister. After he uttered his famous prayer, "Lord, bend me," at a conference in nearby Blaenannerch, he felt overwhelmed by a burden for Welsh souls. His first revival service at Moriah Chapel touched only a handful of people. But crowds began to pour into the church from nearby villages after the Holy Spirit fell on the place in November 1904.

Within a year it was estimated that 100,000 people had come to Christ. Hardened men who normally spent their families' incomes on liquor suddenly were running into the churches and repenting. Coal miners stopped cursing. Teenagers gathered at train stations and sang hymns or testified publicly of their conversions. Crime stopped.

Wales was transformed.

To be fair, it's important to note that the Welsh revival did not revolve around Roberts, at least not in its early days. It was not a man-centered movement—even though newspaper reporters tried to place all the attention on the young preacher. Years before the revival erupted at Moriah Chapel, spiritual birth pangs were felt in other towns in Wales in meetings led by nameless Presbyterian and Salvation Army evangelists who never appeared in newspaper articles. In short, the fervor had been building. An altar had been prepared, and dry wood was waiting for a spark.

That spark happened when Roberts visited Blaenannerch. God took a hot coal from His altar and touched Roberts at age 26. Roberts was gloriously baptized in the Holy Spirit there while others watched him kneeling in a pew. By his own account, he wept so much that three women came over to console him and to wipe the perspiration from his face. The love of God, he said, was boiling inside him.

Roberts described the experience this way: "After many had prayed I felt some living energy or force entering my bosom; it held my breath; my legs trembled terribly; this living energy increased and increased as one after the other prayed until it nearly burst me. . . . I cried—'Bend me, bend me, bend me; Oh! Oh! Oh! Oh! Oh!' . . . What came to mind after this was, the bending in the day of judgment. Then I was filled with sympathy for the people who will have to bend in judgment day, and I wept. Afterwards the salvation of souls weighed heavily on me. I felt on fire for going through the whole of Wales to tell the people about the Saviour."[2]

Two profound characteristics marked the Welsh revival. First, waves of conviction drew people to repentance. Often sinners wandered into the meetings and immediately knelt at the altars. Second, Christians felt an urgency to share Christ with everyone around them because of the reality of hell and God's judgment. They seemed almost possessed by the love of God for the unconverted.

In his meetings Roberts often shared a four-point plan for living the Christian life: (1) confess all known sin, (2) deal with and get rid of anything "doubtful" in your life, (3) be ready to obey the Holy Spirit instantly and (4) confess Christ publicly.

After visiting Moriah Chapel and rereading the accounts of the Welsh revival, I also long for an authentic move of God. I want what Evan Roberts felt in his soul. Yet as I think of what so much of today's movements in the church are known for, I become weary—weary of the fake and the fabricated. We think we have true power. We boast about the size of our crowds. We brag about supposed miracles, though many are not substantiated. We are ready to declare a revival if Christians swoon under the influence of a preacher or give big offerings. But when the music stops, the TV cameras are turned off and the money is counted, what do we have?

Where is the God of Evan Roberts? Where is the true power of God, which can sweep over a city and bring backslidden Christians to repentance and hardened sinners to experience the greatest miracle of all—the miracle of new birth?

We Need the Fire Again

The Bible is full of accounts of people who encountered God's holy fire. When the Lord visited Abram and promised him an heir, "a smoking oven and a flaming torch" appeared (Genesis 15:17). Before Gideon could enter battle, the angel of the Lord appeared to him and consumed the sacrifice with a burning fire (Judges 6:21). Before Elisha began his miraculous ministry, he watched his mentor Elijah rise to heaven amid "a chariot of fire and horses of fire" (2 Kings 2:11). And Isaiah's commissioning occurred after an angelic creature touched his lips with a burning coal from heaven's altar. The prophet's speech was forever transformed.

This is heaven's pattern. God's fire always precedes power. Spiritual revival cannot be generated by man's clever intellect, inspired talent or personal charisma. This is why Jesus told His disciples to wait in Jerusalem for the promise of the Holy Spirit (Luke 24:49). The early Church needed a baptism in the Holy Ghost, even though they had been with Jesus for years, memorized His sermons and witnessed His miracles. That was not enough. They needed more than just a touch on the lips—they needed flames of fire on their heads and a total infilling of *dunamis* power.

No Christian should view the baptism of the Holy Spirit as optional. It is not an experience reserved for an elite few. When Jesus said, "You will receive power when the Holy Spirit has come upon you" (Acts 1:8), He wasn't making a suggestion or offering a single item from a menu in a spiritual cafeteria. He was laying out His divine plan. And there is no Plan B. If the Church ignores the necessity of the baptism in the Spirit we will never fulfill the Great Commission.

The writings of great revivalists from recent centuries reveal they all concur. Not one of them cautioned their followers to avoid the fire of God. They viewed it as a requirement for service.

John Wesley, the founder of the Methodist movement, taught his early followers to seek the baptism of the Holy Spirit. His own experience was marked by what he called "groanings too deep for words," a reference to Spirit-empowered prayer in Romans 8:26. (Some claim that Wesley actually practiced glossolalia, or speaking in tongues, which we will discuss further in Chapter 10, "The Fire of Prayer.")

Founders of the Holiness Movement also emphasized the need for this second baptism. While they did not view speaking in tongues as normative, they urged Christians to "tarry" for the baptism of the Spirit in order to obtain spiritual power over sinful habits—an experience and process they called sanctification. A. B. Simpson, a holiness leader who founded the Christian and Missionary Alliance Church, wrote: "There is no truth that needs to be more emphasized in this age of smartness and human self-sufficiency than the imperative necessity of the baptism in the Holy Spirit as the condition of all effective Christian work. We must tarry before we go."[3]

R. A. Torrey, who helped evangelist D. L. Moody found his Bible college, taught that the baptism in the Spirit was a unique experience, subsequent to conversion: "In regeneration there is an impartation of life, and the one who receives it is saved; in the baptism with the Holy Spirit there is an impartation of power and the one who receives it is fitted for service."[4]

South African revivalist Andrew Murray wrote often of the need for the "second blessing." He constantly reminded believers that conversion to Christ is only the first step into faith. It must be followed by the baptism in the Spirit. "I fear there is a terrible, terrible self-satisfaction among many Christians—they are content with their low level of life. They think they have the Spirit because they are converted, but they know very little of the joy of the Holy Ghost, and of the sanctifying power of the Spirit. . . . Oh, friends, do not be content with that half Christian life that many of you are living, but say, 'God wants it, God commands it; I must be filled with the Spirit.'"[5]

What we know as the Pentecostal revival burst on the scene in 1901 in Kansas and was popularized during the Azusa Street Revival in Los Angeles during 1906–1909. The leader of the Azusa meetings, William Seymour, took the holiness teaching of the Holy Spirit one step further. Here is how he explained it in an early sermon given at Azusa:

> Before Pentecost, the disciples were filled with the unction of the Holy Spirit that sustained them until they received the Holy Ghost baptism. Many people today are filled with joy and gladness, but they are far from the enduement of power. Sanctification brings rest and sweetness and quietness to our souls, for we are one with the Lord Jesus and are able to obey His precious Word, that "Man shall not live by bread alone but by every word that proceedeth out of the mouth of God," and we are feeding upon Christ. But let us wait for the promise of the Father upon our souls, according to Jesus' Word, "John truly baptized with water, but ye shall receive the Holy Ghost not many days hence. . . . Ye shall receive power after that the Holy Ghost is come upon you: and ye shall be witnesses unto me, both in Jerusalem and in all Judea, and in Samaria, and unto the uttermost part of the earth" (Acts 1:8). Glory! Glory! Hallelujah! O worship, get down on your knees and ask the Holy Ghost to come in, and you will find Him right at your heart's door, and He will come in. Prove Him now. Amen.[6]

The Pentecostal movement fueled a surge of missionary activity around the world that continues to this day. Its leaders taught that every Christian must be anointed by the Spirit so he or she can be empowered to do the supernatural work of Christ. Azusa was followed by subsequent moves of the Holy Spirit: the Latter Rain Revival of the 1940s, the healing revival of the 1950s and the charismatic renewal movement that emerged in the 1960s. It could be said that the experience of Pentecost dominated the previous century.

This is why it is surprising that few evangelical Christians today observe the actual Day of Pentecost on the traditional Church calendar. We have a strange way of treating Pentecost, which falls seven weeks after Easter each year. Even those of us who wear the Pentecostal label rarely commemorate it, neglecting to place importance on a date that often gets lost between Mother's Day and Memorial Day.

This is especially odd when we consider that the apostle Paul and the early disciples attached great significance to this date. During his third missionary journey, Paul hurried to reach Jerusalem in time for Pentecost (Acts 20:16), and he told the Corinthians that he planned to stay in Ephesus until Pentecost (1 Corinthians 16:8). Paul had Pentecost on his mind; he marked time with it; it provided a sacred rhythm for his spiritual life. He was, without a doubt, the ultimate Pentecostal.

Before the coming of Christ, Pentecost was a joyful Jewish festival celebrating the wheat harvest fifty days after the first fruits offering. But the Old Covenant version of this holiday was just a foreshadowing of the great spiritual ingathering that would occur after the dramatic outpouring of the Holy Spirit on Jesus' first followers. Pentecost was heaven's inauguration ceremony for the Church, complete with rushing wind, flames of fire and an astounding display of glossolalia. In that moment the men and women gathered in the Upper Room were visibly endued with supernatural power—and three thousand people were converted in response to Peter's Spirit-empowered preaching.

Pentecost was no small miracle. The fire described in Acts 2 was not unlike the fire that fell from heaven on Mount Carmel during Elijah's contest with the prophets of Baal. It came to show us that in the era of grace, God fills frail human vessels with His powerful Spirit— and anoints a new priesthood that is not based on race, gender, age or economic status.

How desperately we need a fresh anointing of Pentecost today. But if we want it, we must go back to the original formula.

Beware of Cheap Substitutes

John the Baptist prophesied that God would endue His Church with power. He also announced that Jesus Christ would give

His Church a double portion of His Spirit. John said: "He [Jesus] will baptize you with the Holy Spirit *and fire*" (Matthew 3:11, emphasis added). When the Day of Pentecost arrived, sure enough, both wind and fire were evident. True Pentecost has both. Let me explain.

We've known the wind during the past forty years of the charismatic movement. We have felt "times of refreshing" in the Holy Spirit's renewing presence. We've enjoyed His healing, basked in His joy, learned about the gifts of the Spirit, claimed His prosperity and received His supernatural power. But I wonder if our experience has been diminished by a selfish focus.

At times we have trivialized Pentecost and made it smaller than it is. We've invited people to come to the altar and receive a slap on the head. Bam! Zap! Take it! We reduce a holy experience to the spiritual equivalent of a fast-food drive-through. We've also turned this experience inward and made it all about us. If we aren't careful, genuine Pentecost can be vulgarized into an emotional frenzy. Some of us have spent a lot of time on the floors of our churches, soaking in His miraculous anointing. We "saturate" and "marinate" in the anointing. We experience "Holy Ghost goose bumps." And sometimes, because of our immaturity, we use the Holy Spirit's power to feed selfish desires or meet emotional wants.

But genuine Pentecost is not just about noise or feelings. John the Baptist said Jesus would baptize us in *fire* as well as *power*. What is the fire of the Spirit?

Fire has a refining element. John the Baptist said: "His winnowing fork is in His hand, and He will thoroughly clear His threshing floor; and He will gather His wheat into the barn, but He will burn up the chaff with unquenchable fire" (Matthew 3:12). When it comes to Pentecost, holiness is not a side issue. It is the essence of the Holy Spirit's work. When He comes in power, He also comes to burn up the sin in our lives. He comes with conviction, searching our motives, uprooting our unforgiveness and shattering our pride.

Our problem is that we treat the whole scene in Acts 2 as if it were a party. We want hoopla instead of the fear of God. We spend our time splashing in the shallow end of His river when He has deeper things for us—things that require godly character and a crucified life. The truth is we are afraid to embrace Jesus' winnowing fork, and we resist when the fire of His Spirit comes to burn up our selfishness.

The Bible says wind and fire appeared on the Day of Pentecost. We will not see Pentecost-style harvest without both. We shouldn't want His anointing without His character.

One subtle way we charismatics cheapen the Holy Spirit's power occurs during altar ministry times in many churches. You probably are familiar with the drill. People line up in the front of the church and ministers lay hands on them, either for healing or for a special anointing. Then, as if on cue, everyone begins to fall on the floor. They have been, as we like to say, "slain in the Spirit."

This practice of slumping onto the floor after receiving prayer, usually into the waiting arms of a "catcher," has become standard in some charismatic churches. This phenomenon represents a powerful and legitimate touch from the Holy Spirit. In view of the sovereignty of God, to deny it would be foolish. Francis MacNutt, a longtime leader in the renewal and one of the foremost authorities on Christian healing, believes that falling under the power can be an extraordinary demonstration of God's power, an intimate experience of His presence, an impetus to repentance or deliverance from evil spirits and an environment for healing. "I find that resting in the Spirit," he writes, "is a marvelous ministry gift that often leads people to experience the love of Jesus, lasting healing and deliverance."[7]

At the same time, this phenomenon can be and often is faked. And we should deplore the counterfeit.

There certainly were times in the Bible when people fell in God's presence or trembled with reverence. In the Old Testament, the priests who ministered in the newly built Temple could not stand because of God's holiness. Demon-possessed people often fell down in the presence of Jesus and His disciples (Mark 9:26; Luke 4:35). The unconverted Saul fell to his knees when he saw the heavenly vision of Christ on the road to Damascus (Acts 9:4; 22:7). And John, the beloved disciple, fell "as though dead" in the presence of the risen Lord Jesus (Revelation 1:17, NIV).

In the first-century church, Ananias and Sapphira also fell down—except they were literally slain by the Spirit (Acts 5:1–11)! They collapsed because the Holy Spirit convicted them of sin (probably inducing a heart attack or stroke). In the ministry of Holiness preacher Maria Woodworth-Etter in the Midwest in the late 1800s, people reportedly "struck down by the power of God" were considered to be under profound conviction for sin. The same was true in the ministries of John Wesley, Jonathan Edwards, Charles G. Finney and others.

When charismatics today are slain in the Spirit, however, it often has nothing to do with conviction. It is generally interpreted as a human response to the anointing of the Holy Spirit, especially relating to healing. Evangelist Kathryn Kuhlman called this "the blessing." In many of her services, hundreds of people fell down simultaneously at a wave of her hand.

Today, falling under the Spirit's power is often considered an experience that should be sought for its own sake. Too often I have watched evangelists send believers tumbling to the floor by brute force, by whacking them on the forehead. The goal seems to be simply to get them to the floor.

At times, when such meetings conclude I overhear people saying to each other, "Wasn't that exciting! God really moved tonight." These comments grieve me. In many cases, nothing profound has been preached from the Scriptures. No one has been converted or healed, although a few say they felt God touch them. Nor do I get the impression that the people who spent so much time on the floor were convicted of sin or more burdened for the lost. It's almost as if we were putting on a show—but whom were we entertaining?

Of course there are times when people respond to the genuine moving of the Spirit, and they may feel overcome by His power. Once when I was praying for people at a crowded altar in Santa Cruz, Bolivia, I could not lay hands on anyone because the government was worried about a swine flu scare. So I prayed for the people from a distance, sometimes just waving my hand over them. In some cases people fell because God's presence was at work.

But we must be cautious in this regard, never flippant or irreverent about the moving of the Spirit, and we must never use the anointing to manipulate a crowd. We must never fake God's power in order to make others feel we are anointed. If we do that, we take something holy and make it common and trivial. And as a result, holy fire becomes something else—a "strange fire" that does not have the power to sanctify.

This very kind of strange fire is spreading today. In some charismatic churches, people take the stage and throw imaginary "fireballs of anointing" at each other, and then fall down, pretending to be slain by the globs of divine power. One young traveling preacher encourages people to inject themselves with pretend needles when they come to the altar, so they can "get high on Jesus." He actually compares being filled with the Spirit to taking cocaine; he also puts a plastic Jesus figurine from a manger scene in his mouth and encourages people to "smoke baby Jesus" so they can experience "Jehovah-juana," a reference to marijuana. This is more serious than trivializing the things of God. This is taking the Lord's name in vain.

I have been in other meetings where women were lying on the floor with their legs spread apart. They were making loud moaning noises and claiming that they were praying and "birthing in the Spirit," as if God would lead them to do something so obscene in a public place.

God help us! We have turned the holy fire of God into a circus sideshow—and naïve Christians are buying this without realizing that such shenanigans are actually blasphemous.

What would the apostle Paul think if he came to some of our shallow "anointing" services? Would he be impressed that people were jerking and shaking on the floor? Would he recognize this as God's genuine fire? What if Andrew Murray visited our meetings, or William Seymour or Charles Finney? Would they find repentance and brokenness, as they expected to see in their day?

My hunch is that these revivalists of the past would denounce such behavior as a gross spiritual counterfeit. They would call us back to the cross, to selflessness, to Christian discipline and to spiritual maturity. And they would rebuke us for being spiritual babies who want entertainment instead of responsibility.

When I read the account of the Welsh revival of 1904, I picture a pure outpouring of God's Spirit that was not fabricated or defiled. I feel the same when I read of the early days of Azusa Street, where blacks, whites and Hispanics worshiped together in early morning prayer to seek God and true sanctification.

We need another outpouring of God's fire, one that is not corrupted by cheap antics. If you have been involved in some form of counterfeit spirituality, I urge you to repent of your carnal cravings and ask God for a fresh infilling of His Spirit. Stop seeking a Band-Aid for your soul and let the Holy Ghost take His winnowing fork all the way to the root of your selfish nature. Ask Him for a fresh Pentecost—one that is not just for power but for holiness as well.

Questions for Discussion

1. What happened to the church on the Day of Pentecost?
2. Describe your own personal Pentecost, if you have had such an experience.

3. What are the two works the Holy Spirit does in our lives when we are baptized in the Holy Spirit (Matthew 3:11–12)?

4. Sometimes people shake, fall, laugh or cry when the Holy Spirit touches them. Has this ever happened to you? Have you ever "faked" any of these experiences? If so, how do you think God views this?

I was with you in weakness and in fear and in much trembling, and my message and my preaching were not in persuasive words of wisdom, but in demonstration of the Spirit and of power, so that your faith would not rest on the wisdom of men, but on the power of God.

1 Corinthians 2:3–5

No man is fitted for the humblest service in the Church of God until he receives the divine baptism of the Holy Spirit. The mother needs it in the nursery, the Sunday school teacher in his class, the preacher in his pulpit, the soul winner in his dealings with the inquirer and the saint in the ministry of prayer in the secret closet. There is no truth that needs to be more emphasized in this age of smartness and human self-sufficiency than the imperative necessity of the baptism of the Holy Spirit as the condition of all effective Christian work. We must tarry before we go.

A. B. Simpson, founder of
the Christian and Missionary
Alliance Church (1843–1919)[1]

2

The Fire of Supernatural Anointing

During my 26 years as a journalist I've interviewed many interesting people and heard some amazing stories. But a new standard was set in 2007 when I met two people in southern India who had experienced biblical-style resurrection.

Six-year-old Jyothi Pothabathula looked like a typical girl from Andhra Pradesh, a state in southern India. She had wide brown eyes, mocha-colored skin, slick dark hair and a shy smile. When I asked her who brought her back to life when she was two years old, she demurely answered, "Jesus," in her native Telugu language.

"In May 2004, we were coming to the evangelistic crusade on a bus when she collapsed," Jyothi's father, Suribabu, told me during a chat in my hotel room. The little girl had no history of illness, but she had suddenly stopped breathing during the bumpy ride. The girl's mother, Nagamani, said she began desperately praying for God to save her baby.

Suribabu and his wife were traveling to the town of Kakinada to attend an outreach festival sponsored by Harry Gomes, an evangelist based in the southern Indian city of Coimbatore. When the couple arrived at the event with Jyothi's lifeless body in her father's arms, someone urged them to push through the crowd to reach the stage where Gomes was praying for the sick.

They quickly carried the girl to the preacher. Immediately after Gomes prayed for her, they said, Jyothi sat up and then began walking. The crowd erupted in applause.

"I know Jesus is a great God because He raised my daughter to life," Suribabu told me, wiping away tears. He was already a new Christian when the miracle occurred. His brother and two more of his Hindu family members converted to Jesus after they heard the story and saw the revived girl.

In late 2006, Mesheck Manepally, a 45-year-old shop owner, was attending one of Gomes's meetings in Prathipadu, another city in Andhra Pradesh. Mesheck's son, Varaprasad, said his father collapsed in the back of the crowd and began foaming at the mouth. Varaprasad was hysterical, but he managed to flag down an emergency vehicle so he could take his dad to a hospital.

When crusade organizers learned of the emergency and alerted Gomes, he interrupted his preaching, left the stage and walked to the side of the crowd, which had swelled to 100,000. By that time, Gomes said, Mesheck had no pulse and showed other signs of death, including a dark pallor and stiffness of the body.

Gomes laid his hands on the man and prayed for his life to return. Within a few minutes, Mesheck sat up in the back of the vehicle with a dazed look on his face. "People started telling me, 'You were dead and now you are alive!'" Mesheck said. "I was confused and I started crying. I was so thankful."

Mesheck's wife, Laxmi, said that for ten days after the incident Hindus from her village came to visit her husband. "They viewed him as a Lazarus," she said. "The people were saying, 'Their God is the true God.'"

Since medical documentation is not easily available in isolated, rural areas of India, skeptics may argue that these miracles can't be confirmed. Death certificates weren't issued in either case, and no doctors were on hand to verify the facts.

But Jyothi's parents and Mesheck's family say that doesn't negate what they know is true.

Gomes believes God is displaying His power in India today in dramatic ways in order to draw Hindus to Jesus Christ. As this book went to print, he had witnessed five incidents of resurrection in his meetings since he began conducting evangelistic crusades in 1996. "Every time it happens it boosts the people's faith," Gomes said. "In the Bible we are told that the crowds came not just to see Jesus but to see Lazarus. As the word about these miracles spreads, everyone's faith is elevated."

The Missing Axe Head

I've witnessed these types of New Testament miracles often during my travels in developing countries. God's power is at work in amazing ways in Asia, Africa and Latin America.

During a visit to Punjab, in northern India, in 2005, I met Pastor Howell, a sixty-year-old man who had planted more than three hundred churches in seven years. Also the founder of a Bible college, Pastor Howell asked me to come to a church he had started two days earlier in a rural village. I was curious about a church that was only two days old.

As we drove to the isolated town on a crude dirt road, he explained to me how he started the church after praying for a girl who was dying of a heart ailment. Her parents were devout Hindus, but when Pastor Howell prayed for her in the hospital and she recovered within minutes, the parents told him they wanted to serve his God. He led them to Christ, then they destroyed their Hindu idols and invited the whole village to hear their daughter's testimony. The night I came to their home, more than 45 people were sitting on rugs in the front yard to experience their first church meeting. All of them converted to Christ because they saw evidence of one healing miracle.

In 2006 I visited one of the most dynamic evangelical churches in Cairo, Egypt. The missions director told me an amazing story of how God was using miracles to reach the Muslims of his nation. He said that because the government did not allow his church to openly preach the Gospel, he and other church members operated a mobile medical clinic in villages in southern Egypt.

Recently, he said, the Christians tacked posters all over one Muslim village announcing the date and time when the mobile clinic would be passing through. When the team arrived the next morning there was a long line of people waiting to see a nurse or doctor. Many of those seeking treatment were fully veiled women. When the first woman was admitted into the one-room clinic, the nurse asked her what kind of physical ailment she had.

"The woman said she did not have a physical problem, but that she had had a dream about Jesus Christ, and she wondered if we could explain this to her," the Cairo pastor told me. "So we gave her an Arabic Bible and told her about Jesus." He said the next woman in line also admitted that she had dreamed about Christ and wanted to talk to a Christian about it. The women who took the Bibles slipped them under their *hijabs* and walked away.

"This went on all day!" the pastor said. "God is visiting Muslims in their sleep and revealing Jesus to them. This is opening huge doors to advance the Gospel."

This type of subjective supernatural experience does not fit in anyone's intellectual grid. You can't figure it out, quantify it, program it or predict it. God's miraculous ways are higher than our ways. And one miracle can do more to advance Christ's Kingdom than a million words of man's wisdom.

In 2001 I spent more than a week with leaders of China's underground house church movement. All of these amazingly humble men and women had been in prison at least three times each, and many had been beaten by police with iron crowbars. Yet they were the most joyful Christians I have ever met. And all of them had experienced miracles.

One day I gathered some of the leaders in my hotel room for an off-the-record interview. When I asked the men what was the most remarkable miracle they had ever seen, they all began to laugh and talk to each other in rapid Chinese. There was such a commotion! I asked my translator why they were so excited. He told me, "They find it difficult to tell you which miracle is the greatest. There are so many!"

I thought to myself: *I wish we had this problem in the United States—too many miracles!*

Finally all the men stopped talking and deferred to an elderly man they called "Uncle." They respected him because of his age and because he had suffered so much persecution for his faith during Mao Zedong's crackdown on Christianity in the 1970s. The man then told how he led many people to Christ in one village after an unusual incident of resurrection.

"This lady came to me for prayer, and she was holding a dead baby in her arms," the man said. "At first I was intimidated, but I just put my hand on the cold corpse and prayed a simple prayer. Within a few minutes the baby began to cough. And then, everyone there became Christian!"

Why is it that these types of miracles are more common overseas? Surely the Holy Spirit does not operate by different rules on American soil. Yet it does seem that faith for the supernatural is higher in cultures where people are less encumbered by Western-style intellectualism. Just as the climate of unbelief prevented Jesus from doing "many miracles" in his hometown of Nazareth (Matthew 13:58), it seems we have created a religious climate in our country that is not conducive to miracle faith.

Scripture tells us that during Elisha's ministry, one of the prophet's sons dropped the head of his axe into the Jordan River while cutting a tree (2 Kings 6:1–7). When Elisha was called to help recover it, he threw a stick in the river and the axe head floated to the surface. Because of the miraculous anointing of the Holy Spirit, iron floated on water. Something physically impossible became possible.

How desperately we need to raise this axe head from the water today! It is as if we have lost the miraculous. In fact some Christians in the United States teach a doctrine called cessationism that suggests miracles stopped altogether after the Bible was canonized. Likewise, many churches teach that God, in a sense, flipped a switch in heaven and shut down His supernatural power after the first apostles died. Cessationists are content to do ministry merely with sermons, seminaries and church programs, even though they acknowledge they still need the Holy Spirit to win souls.

I believe this is why so much of American Christianity is impotent. We cannot claim New Testament results because we do not preach a New Testament Gospel. We have diluted the message and stripped it of power. We simply don't expect the book of Acts to mirror our experience.

Where today is the God of the early apostles? Where is the God of Elisha? To answer this, we may need to ask: Where in our midst is the God of the underground Chinese church? Here in the West we have lost our axe head and have tried cutting wood with only the handle. No one can fell trees or cut wood with an axe handle. You must have the blade.

The sharp anointing of New Testament faith is still available, but it must be recovered from where we dropped it—in the murky, dark abyss of doubt, religious tradition and intellectual pride. We must return to the Jordan River—the place where the Holy Spirit descended like a dove upon Jesus and anointed Him for ministry. We must receive a fresh baptism. Only there can we receive power from the Spirit to advance the Kingdom of God.

Discerning True and False Miracles

Genuine miracles have a profound impact. Moses needed only one burning-bush experience in the desert before agreeing to deliver his fellow Jews out of Egyptian bondage. When Jesus

56

peered into the soul of the Samaritan woman and named her troubled past, that one miracle led to the conversion of an entire village. When one lame beggar lying at the Temple gate suddenly began to walk, an entire city watched; Peter's sermon following that miracle led to two thousand conversions.

While it is imperative that we reclaim the miraculous, it is also important that we distance ourselves from the phony, the fake and the occult. We cannot be so famished for the supernatural that we naïvely open the door to deception or spiritual scams. God never called us to *chase* miracles; on the contrary, He said miracles should *follow* us (Mark 16:17–18).

Some charismatics have adopted the notion that miraculous signs and wonders are supposed to occur at the drop of a hat or on a daily basis, as if we can conjure them at will. This thinking is dangerous. If we become so hungry for the supernatural that we throw caution to the wind, we will find ourselves ingesting things that are toxic. We must remember that not all forms of supernatural power are from God. Pharaoh had magicians in his court who mimicked God's signs and wonders. Satan has angels of false light who can work false miracles.

Jesus warned His disciples that charlatans would use spiritual gifts as a disguise while they preyed upon the naïve:

> Watch out for false prophets. They come to you in sheep's clothing, but inwardly they are ferocious wolves. By their fruit you will recognize them. . . . Not everyone who says to me, "Lord, Lord," will enter the kingdom of heaven, but only he who does the will of my Father who is in heaven. Many will say to me on that day, "Lord, Lord, did we not prophesy in your name, and in your name drive out demons and perform many miracles?" Then I will tell them plainly, "I never knew you. Away from me, you evildoers!"
>
> Matthew 7:15–16, 21–23, NIV

Outwardly, false prophets bear an amazing resemblance to the real thing. But on the inside, Jesus said, they are "ferocious wolves," and their hidden motive is to steal money or attention from the flock of God.

Jesus did not say these men actually healed the sick or cast out demons. Some of these imposters may have operated in demonic power. Others may simply have *claimed* they performed miracles in order to attract a following, and the possibility exists that they did not. It is no different today.

Let's never forget that the same apostle Paul who healed many sick people also rebuked a false prophet named Elymas (or Bar-Jesus) and caused him to go blind temporarily (Acts 13:6–11). Paul told this Jewish magician: "You who are full of all deceit and fraud, you son of the devil, you enemy of all righteousness, will you not cease to make crooked the straight ways of the Lord?" (verse 10).

Although the disciples in the book of Acts had access to miracles, signs and wonders, they had no tolerance for spiritual fraud. Paul and his disciples could smell spiritual counterfeits a mile away. They knew that if false prophets, false apostles, false teachers or spiritual con artists were allowed to flourish in the New Testament church, the Gospel would be poisoned and God's people would be misled.

Jesus did not offer His warning to make us suspicious of healing or other spiritual gifts. He Himself healed the sick and performed miracles, and His disciples raised the dead by God's power. If we believe the message of the New Testament, then we will accept prophecy, miracles and healings (as recorded in 1 Corinthians 12) as genuine expressions of the Holy Spirit's anointing.

Jesus' warning in Matthew 7 was not intended to scare us away from the gifts of the Spirit. We need the genuine. But He was alerting us to the fact that imposters will attempt to hide their true motives behind a facade of spirituality, and He was exhorting us to use discernment.

We have sorely needed it. The charismatic movement in America has produced its share of pretenders like Elymas. We've had healing evangelists who were con artists. We've had so-called prophets who prophesy with eloquence and the proper intonation yet their message was a sham. Others have used deception to convince audiences of their divine giftings. I want to give you a striking example.

Lying Prophets and Fake Healers

The charismatic movement lost much in terms of credibility during the past few decades because we allowed imposters and charlatans to thrive in our midst. Some of these people started out with good intentions; many of them surely were anointed by the Holy Spirit's power in the beginning. But somewhere along the way, like Esau, they traded their birthright for a meager bowl of stew. They became enamored by the publicity or the big offerings, and before long any divine anointing they once had faded into a dim aura of self-importance.

Such was the case with Paul Cain, a prophet who was celebrated by charismatics during the 1980s and 1990s. Cain needed no introduction when he stepped up to the podium at a large charismatic conference I was attending in Texas in 1989. Everyone in the audience that evening had heard the astounding stories of this man's prophetic prowess, and many in the crowd were hoping to see and hear his spiritual gifts in action. The atmosphere was charged with nervous antici-pation as Cain finished his sermon and began his practice of calling out individuals by name and delivering uniquely tailored messages from the Lord.

The nervousness was understandable. It was reported that when Cain had spoken at a conference sponsored by Vineyard Ministries International in Anaheim, California, a strange power surge had occurred, short-circuiting a video camera and telephone system. Many people attending that conference had taken this as a sign of the Holy Spirit's power, and Cain began to be viewed by some charismatics as a forerunner of a coming revival of New Testament–style miracles.

Indeed, the stories circulating about Paul Cain had already set him in a class by himself. Prior to his birth, his sickly mother is said to have been visited by an angel who told her that her baby would grow up to preach the Gospel in the manner of the apostle Paul. She was subsequently healed of four major illnesses, according to Cain's testimony.

Cain typically told his audiences that at age eight he was visited by the same angel and commissioned to preach and heal the sick. From 1947 to 1958, he ministered in Pentecostal tent crusades during the heyday of revivalists Oral Roberts, William Branham and A. A. Allen. He was famous in certain circles for his reputed ability to identify by name perfect strangers in a crowd. He would often call people out, then proceed to name their secret transgressions.

Cain came to be viewed as a modern-day Nathan, pointing his finger at guilty sinners and hypocrites. At the same time, he was said to be repulsed by the pride and greed associated with many healing ministries of the 1950s. So Cain reportedly decided not to return to the pulpit until he identified "a new breed" of humble, young church leaders.

With all this background, none of us who had gathered at the San Antonio Convention Center knew quite what to expect. The lights might go out. Television cameras might blow up. A prominent pastor might be humiliated publicly. There might even be an earthquake, since a story was circulating that Cain had accurately predicted a minor trembler in southern California earlier that year. But whatever would transpire, most of us seated in the auditorium believed that Cain was a special messenger from God equipped with divine power.

Nothing earthshaking took place that evening. After his sermon, Cain delivered prophecies to about ten individuals or couples. Each of the messages was laced with bits of personal data—first names, cities, street numbers.

To one pastor and his wife, personal friends of mine, Cain mentioned the number 4001 (their church office was located at 4001 Newberry Road) and predicted they would experience great revival in their Florida city. At another point, Cain asked if "Mark and Debbie" from Washington, D.C., were in the audience. This couple had pastored a church in Washington for several years with a ministry office located at 139 C Street, near the U.S. Capitol. "There's something about 139 C," Cain said, and he proceeded to predict that spiritual revival would someday impact Capitol Hill.

Most people left the meeting that night astounded at the remarkable demonstration of the words of knowledge in Paul Cain's prophecies. It seemed that Cain had literally "read these people's mail" by recounting personal information he could not have known about total strangers. But I found myself struggling.

I had no reason to doubt Cain's sincerity. He seemed like a humble man. But it disturbed me that many who received these prophetic directives were part of the full-time staff of the ministry sponsoring the conference. It also seemed puzzling that all the information Cain ostensibly received from God (mostly street numbers) was printed in a staff address directory that I knew was easily available to conference speakers. Surely Cain would not have studied that list prior to the meeting, then "recalled" the names and numbers to make us think he had revelatory powers! I dismissed the thought.

A year later, my questions resurfaced. If this man were a true prophet from God, most of his prophecies would be coming true, wouldn't they? I began to conduct my own research.

The majority of the personal messages Cain had conveyed that December evening, I discovered, had "fallen to the ground," coming up empty. The church on 4001 Newberry Road, for example, had closed and most of the members had left the city, including the pastor and his wife (who eventually divorced). "Mark and Debbie" resigned their pastoral positions in Washington, D.C., the 139 C Street office was rented to another group and the church moved to the suburbs.

Another young man—who had been told by Cain he would orchestrate a fruitful ministry in southern California—told me he had moved to Texas.

A missionary who received a word from Cain that night later left the mission field disillusioned. Another man who was called out of the crowd had a moral failure about ten years later. I had serious questions: *Is this the way prophecy is supposed to work?*

Several years after that meeting, I interviewed Paul Cain. He insisted during our conversation that he did not obtain information from any source other than God. When I asked why the prophecies did not come true, he said he was depressed during that time period because of his mother's death, and therefore his predictions were inaccurate.

For quite a few years after this, prominent leaders in the charismatic renewal continued to endorse Cain's ministry and vouch for his character. But I could not ignore the fact that most of the prophecies he gave in that meeting in 1989 were off-base. It was unsettling to me that we allowed Cain such free access to churches when there were fundamental questions about the fruit of his ministry.

The rest of the story didn't surface until 2004, when three charismatic leaders who had played a large role in giving Cain a platform brought serious moral charges against him. Mike Bickle, Rick Joyner and Jack Deere posted their grievances on the Internet, accusing Cain of a pattern of alcoholism and homosexuality. Cain initially denied the charges. But just before I was about to go public with a story in *Charisma* about the situation, he faxed a confession statement acknowledging that the accusations were true. He agreed to step down from ministry to receive counseling.

The whole story was painfully devastating to the charismatic movement. Why? Because leaders had not only endorsed this man but made him out to be a special oracle of God. In the end, when the truth emerged, it became clear that Cain had serious moral and ethical problems.

For many people, these last-minute realizations were too late. They had built their Christian experience on this man's words. Now they didn't know what to believe. The rug had been pulled out from under them. Their very foundations were shaky. They became disillusioned or cynical. Some people began to question everything—even the ability of God's people to hear His voice.

How can we protect ourselves from imposters while at the same time promoting the healthy flow of the supernatural gifts of the Holy Spirit in our churches? What could we learn from the case of Paul Cain? I would recommend the following.

1. Don't deify human beings. Thousands of Christians had put Cain on a pedestal, where no man or woman belongs. People expected him almost to be like God. It was a setup for disappointment—and ultimate failure.

We charismatics are prone to deifying preachers. If someone occasionally experiences the gift of miracles in his ministry, we want to make him into a god. The people of Lystra assumed that Paul and Barnabas were gods because they had healed a lame man (Acts 14:11–12). The residents of Malta said the same of Paul because God healed him of a deadly snakebite (Acts 28:6). In both cases Paul rejected the suggestion and insisted he was only a man. Today, I fear, some church leaders are not so quick to dismiss it when they are mistaken for deity.

2. Don't elevate anointing over character. When Paul instructed Timothy to choose leaders for the churches he had planted, he gave him a long list of qualifications. None of these had anything to do with supernatural anointing. Paul did not tell Timothy to choose men who could heal the sick, raise the dead or interpret dreams and visions. In fact, the only anointing he required was the ability to teach the Scriptures.

What Paul required most was Christian morality and character. He told his spiritual son to choose men who were faithful to their wives, temperate, prudent, respectable, hospitable, gentle, peaceable, not greedy, not pugnacious and able to manage their families (1 Timothy 3:2–7). Women leaders,

63

also, were to be examples of character (verse 11). What this shows us is that while spiritual gifts are needed for the advancement of the Kingdom, they don't authorize people to be out front. Just because a person has a powerful anointing doesn't mean they should be given a role of influence in the church. Their gifting must be accompanied by character.

3. Dismiss the sensational. The Holy Spirit always acts according to godly character. He is not schizophrenic. "The fruit of the Spirit is love, joy, peace, patience, kindness, goodness, faithfulness, gentleness, [and] self-control" (Galatians 5:22–23). This means if the Holy Spirit is manifesting Himself in a miraculous way through signs and wonders, He will not contradict these attributes.

Some flashy healing evangelists love to swagger on stage, prancing around like peacocks while they call people to their platforms for prayer. These men are grieving the Spirit of God. The Spirit does not call attention to man, nor does He bless arrogance. He resists the proud—so you can be sure God is nowhere near this cocky display.

I've also seen these same evangelists smacking people on the head and causing them to "fall under the anointing." They believe that the number of bodies on the floor indicates the level of the Holy Spirit's power. This, too, is a mockery. The Spirit is gentle. In actuality, the Spirit is often grieved in situations like this because people are being misled, manipulated and mistreated as they are thrown around onstage. (This is not to mention the manipulation of the audience.)

In 2008, Canadian revivalist Todd Bentley held a four-month series of nightly meetings in Lakeland, Florida, that came to be known as the Lakeland Revival. Bentley was controversial from the beginning, not necessarily because of his tattoos and body piercings but because he was known to shove his knee into people's chests and shout "Bam!" when he prayed for them. Critics also dismissed Bentley's outlandish healing claims because his staff never produced documented evidence of the miracles.

Bentley received much international attention through nightly broadcasts of the meetings on a Christian television channel. He himself often described the event as the greatest revival in world history. The revival and miracle reports were so hyped that Bentley could not live up to the grand expectations. Sadly, the whole phenomenon ended in disgrace when Bentley left his wife and married a younger woman.

Again, Scripture gives us a clear example of warning. When the Holy Spirit was first poured out on the Samaritans, a magician named Simon offered Peter and the other apostles money in exchange for the spiritual power that was in operation. Peter rebuked him for his wickedness (Acts 8:18–24). Simon's sin is still obvious today. When carnal man gets involved in the miraculous ministry of the Spirit, he will try to sensationalize it, bottle it and sell it. We should never support this kind of charismatic circus sideshow.

4. Teach and practice discernment. Discernment is a gift of the Holy Spirit (1 Corinthians 12:10). This means the ability to discern is also a supernatural grace. Therefore we cannot avoid deception without the Holy Spirit's supernatural work among us. Discernment is something we learn by experience as our spiritual senses are trained.

The apostle John told his followers: "Beloved, do not believe every spirit, but test the spirits to see whether they are from God, because many false prophets have gone out into the world" (1 John 4:1). The word *test* here is the same as *assay*, the process of melting metal to find out its content. This means that even when something looks like gold, it may actually be a cheap alloy.

I knew a pastor who invited a Brazilian woman minister to speak at his church in Canada. The woman claimed to perform many healings in her ministry. She also had a more exotic manifestation: Golden dust would sometimes appear on her hair and body as she preached. People saw this as a sign of the Holy Spirit's presence and power.

But the discerning pastor decided to put 1 John 4:1 into practice—literally. He asked some people who had been in this woman's meetings to bring some of the golden dust to him so that he could have it analyzed. He sent it to a metallurgy lab and it was proven to be plastic flakes! Needless to say, this pastor canceled the meeting and told the woman she was not welcome to minister. He protected his church from spiritual pollution.

Discernment is manifested by a "knowing"—a deep, gut-level sense that something is off-base. I think of it as a Holy Spirit–inspired warning system. Spiritually mature people who have tuned their discernment through prayer and Bible study often get a strong sense when something is wrong about a teaching, a relationship or a life situation. This is not the human emotion of suspicion—which operates by fear, resentment or cynicism. True discernment operates by love, in order to protect people from spiritual danger.

Oftentimes when a church is exposed to a false prophet or a con artist, and the minister is later exposed as a fraud, people will admit they had a "weird feeling" when he first showed up. But because everyone jumped on the proverbial bandwagon, and church leaders gave the minister some form of endorsement, those who initially discerned a problem ignored their inner witness. Don't ignore the Holy Spirit! If we would obey His promptings in the beginning there would be no crisis in the end.

5. Enforce accountability. Because so many charismatics left their established denominations and developed a distaste for religious control, we now have the opposite problem: Our movement is too independent. Many traveling ministers in charismatic circles pride themselves for their "freedom in the Spirit," yet some use it as a license to extort money and peddle fraudulent claims.

I know of one freelance "revivalist" who engaged in numerous immoral affairs with women as he traveled around the country. He had no ministry board and no accountability structure. He answered to no one. And yet pastors allowed him in their pulpits without asking questions. They didn't find out until he had left town that he slept with women in the church while he was prophesying over people and laying his hands on them at the altars.

We must stop this cavalier style of ministry. Ministers who refuse to submit to standards of accountability are spiritual renegades—and God says rebellion is the same as the sin of witchcraft. They are what the apostle Jude called "hidden reefs" and "clouds without water" (Jude 12) and are compared both to Korah, who led an unsuccessful rebellion against Moses, and Balaam, a warlock who was paid to prophesy.

Jude makes it clear that people who invade the Church on false pretenses for their own gain, or to corrupt it with fraud and heresy, are "devoid of the Spirit" (verse 19). They may claim to have an anointing from God, but the Spirit of Truth testifies against them that they are charlatans and deceivers who will inherit heaven's judgment.

We must reclaim New Testament power, but we must also develop true discernment and the right accountability systems to avoid the pitfalls of the past. May God visit us with a fresh fire of genuine miracles that draw sinners to repentance and fill the church with holy awe.

Questions for Discussion

1. Why do you think miracles are more common in churches in the developing world?
2. Why is it so important for the Church to recover the "missing axe head" of supernatural anointing?
3. Have you ever been influenced by a false prophet, or by someone who either faked miracles or used the occult to counterfeit them? Why is it important for Christians to guard the Church from these imposters?
4. Why is character more important than spiritual anointing?
5. What is the purpose of the Spirit's gift of discernment?

And when they had prayed, the place where they had gathered together was shaken, and they were all filled with the Holy Spirit and began to speak the word of God with boldness.

Acts 4:31

Here am I, send me; send me to the ends of the earth; send me to the rough, the savage pagans of the wilderness; send me from all that is called comfort on earth; send me even to death itself, if it be but in Thy service, and to promote Thy kingdom.

David Brainerd, missionary to
Native Americans (1718–1747)[1]

Many people are naturally shy. They long to do something for Christ, but they are afraid. The Holy Spirit can make you bold if you will look to Him and trust Him to do it. It was He who turned cowardly Peter into the one who fearlessly faced the Sanhedrin and rebuked their sin.

R. A. Torrey, American revivalist (1856–1928)[2]

My main ambition in life is to be on the Devil's most wanted list.

Leonard Ravenhill, author
and preacher (1907–1994)[3]

3

The Fire of Boldness

We all have heroes. Since I was a young Christian, the Dutch evangelist Brother Andrew has been my role model from afar. Ever since I read his book *God's Smuggler*, in which he narrated the adventure of sneaking Bibles into dangerous Eastern European countries in the Communist era, I have admired his spiritual courage. I learned from Brother Andrew that Christianity, at its core, is about taking the fire of God where people and the devil don't want us to go.

When I began my traveling ministry in 2001 I discovered that there are literally thousands of Brother Andrews all over the planet. I find these humble heroes in places such as India, Nigeria, Egypt, Bolivia and China. These simple people have stirred me to the depths of my soul—and their examples have revealed to me a shameful lack of courage in the comfortable American church.

Kelechi is one of my bravest African friends. He started a ministry in Nigeria a few years ago that focuses on evangelizing vicious militant gangs. Some of these paramilitary groups have kidnapped oil company workers in Nigeria's petroleum-rich delta region. But Kelechi is not afraid of their guns or machetes. In fact, he has allowed himself to be kidnapped in order to have face-to-face conversations with gang leaders.

Kelechi also trains college students to reach the leaders of Nigeria's campus "cults." These mysterious fraternal organizations are involved in occult rituals, including at times human sacrifice. Yet Kelechi and his friends risk their lives every day to share Christ with these people.

I met 29-year-old Jeet during a trip to northern India in 2007. His Hindu father disowned him when he became a Christian at age seventeen. "My father said that if I deny Jesus I can come back," Jeet told me with a resolute tone. He has never returned to his parents' home.

Jeet has a slight frame, but his heart is ablaze with courage. He has been planting churches in two of India's most resistant states, Bihar and Orissa. In 2006, a group of Hindu fanatics attacked him and ordered him to stop his meetings. They also threatened to kill one of his colleagues. "They told me there is no need to preach the Gospel here," Jeet said, "but I tell them it is a commandment from Jesus to preach to all people."

I met Otoniel, a Guatemalan pastor, in 2003 during my first mission trip to his country. "Pastor Oto" lives in an area that was deeply scarred by Guatemala's 36-year civil war. After he was baptized in the Holy Spirit, he planted a church in 1980 in the town of El Rosario. The growing congregation has become a beacon of hope to a needy region.

Today, from his modest, three-bedroom house, Pastor Oto feeds lunch to most of the poor children in his town, operates an orphanage and a vocational training center, and preaches the Gospel on the radio daily. "One day we will go to other nations and spread the Gospel," Oto told me.

Jeyasingh is a brave Indian woman who refuses to fit in anyone's box. In a nation where women still suffer unimaginable discrimination and abuse, she has worked tirelessly as a leader among India's growing Pentecostal churches. Now 54,

Jeyasingh trains young pastors from her isolated school in the state of Bihar, in northern India, where Hindu tradition is strong. She is particularly motivated to train more women; those who convert to Christianity struggle to learn the Bible because they have been denied education.

I saw a fire in Jeyasingh's eyes that I don't see often in my own country. It was a mix of holy courage and relentless love. "This whole nation will be set ablaze," she said of India's future.

Xuan is a church planter in rural China. I met him at a secret training conference held near Hong Kong seven years ago. He told me how militant Buddhists used medieval swords to attack him when he tried to evangelize an area of northern China a few years earlier. During the conference he saved soaps and shampoos from his hotel room to take on his missionary journeys. He had no money, but his faith was big—even though he knew he might spend some time in prison for that faith.

These people are my heroes. They have denied themselves to take up the cross. They endure persecution from government officials, angry villagers and family members, because they live, eat and breathe one passion: to make Christ known to a broken world.

They have experienced the fire of Pentecost—and in their case the fire seems to have propelled them into a place of boldness we don't experience in America. They are stretching their meager resources to feed orphans while we attend "financial breakthrough" seminars; they are being arrested for their ministry activities while we seek more creature comforts. And they are risking their necks to preach to the lost in their countries while we question whether we are "called" to evangelize.

Why Are We Baptized in the Spirit?

It's clear from the New Testament that the anointing of the Holy Spirit on the Day of Pentecost had a practical purpose.

Jesus told His disciples that the Spirit would empower them so they could preach "both in Jerusalem, and in all Judea and Samaria, and even to the remotest part of the earth" (Acts 1:8). We also see in Matthew 3:11–12 that the baptism in the Spirit enables us to live a sanctified life. The Spirit both empowers us and sanctifies us; He inflames us with zeal and refines us in holiness.

Jesus introduced the concept of Spirit-empowered evangelism when He read from the scroll that had been opened that day in the synagogue. He announced, quoting the prophet Isaiah, "The Spirit of the Lord is upon Me, because *He has anointed Me to preach the gospel to the poor.* He has sent Me to proclaim release to the captives, and recovery of sight to the blind, to set free those who are oppressed, to proclaim the favorable year of the Lord" (Luke 4:18–19, emphasis added).

Jesus was emphasizing that His primary mission was an evangelistic one. Even though He fulfilled many ministry functions, "preaching the Gospel to the poor" was primary. And He said this was the ultimate reason He was anointed by the Spirit!

So it should be with us. While the Holy Spirit enables us to do many things, and distributes many spiritual gifts to the Church, including healing, teaching, prophecy, tongues, miracles and more, the core purpose for the anointing of the Spirit is evangelism. Yet I wonder: Do we share this priority?

When the early disciples were filled with the Spirit a second time (the infilling of the Spirit should be continual) the Bible says there was one clear manifestation: boldness. "And when they had prayed, the place where they had gathered together was shaken, and they were all filled with the Holy Spirit and began to speak the word of God with boldness" (Acts 4:31). Notice that in this passage, speaking in tongues and prophecy are not mentioned. The outstanding manifestation of the Spirit was a supernatural courage that gives people a special grace to speak for God.

We need this fire today!

I recently watched a vintage Billy Graham sermon from his 1971 crusade at McCormick Place in Chicago. I chuckled at the shag haircuts, huge afros and bright polyester fabrics on display in the audience. Everything looked so dated, and the music performed before the sermon was almost prehistoric. The cultural references included a mention of the rock opera *Jesus Christ Superstar* and a remark about the band Ocean's 1970 hippie ballad, "Put Your Hand in the Hand." Talk about nostalgia!

But when Graham held his Bible in the air and preached about the uniqueness of Jesus Christ in that packed arena, nothing seemed outdated. The sermon might as well have been recorded yesterday. His message, in fact, seemed more relevant than a lot of the Christian books, videos, blogs and PowerPoint-enhanced teachings we circulate today.

Listening to Graham stirs something deep inside me: a passion to preach and to see the American church set ablaze with a passion for the Gospel. How we need to return to the simplicity of evangelism that cuts to the heart, produces repentance and reveals the Son of God.

The charismatic community is in desperate need of reclaiming the ministry of evangelism. In the early 1970s, during the Jesus Movement era, we seemed to have soul-winning as a priority. Yet as we moved into the 1980s and 1990s, we began emphasizing the need for apostles and prophets. Initially I cheered this movement because I believe we should reclaim every spiritual gift in the New Testament that has been avoided or neglected.

We need apostles and prophets because they keep the church moving forward in our global assignment and provide heavenly direction and strategy. Yet the mere concept of apostles and prophets has been controversial in our time, not only because certain corners of the Church reject them on theological grounds, but because some self-proclaimed apostles and hypermystical prophets have abused and misused their gifts and authority. Some of these ministers have slipped over the edge of orthodoxy—and in some instances have taken segments of the Church over the cliff with them.

Some charismatic leaders have promoted the concept that apostles are spiritual supermen who have the authority to wield rigid, hierarchical control over churches and leaders— a notion that has resulted in authoritarianism and abuse. Others have perverted the apostolic model to create a financial "downline" that brings loads of money to a few at the top of the food chain—ignoring the Bible's injunction that apostles should be models of humility who serve from the bottom. Meanwhile, some prophets have traded in their originally pure message to promote bizarre doctrines and cryptic predictions that often prove to be hokum.

Is it possible that while we've been celebrating "super apostles" and building fan clubs for prophets we have ignored the primacy of our evangelistic calling?

In this turbulent season when our movement is being shaken, refined and redefined, we must return to the simplicity of our mission to reach the lost all around us. God wants to visit us with fresh evangelistic fire that will burn up our selfishness, refocus our priorities, rid us of quirky doctrinal distractions and ignite our hearts with a holy love for people who don't know Jesus.

Take It to the Streets

East Monument Street in downtown Baltimore's east side is not far from the city's gleaming Inner Harbor district. But the neighborhood I visited in 2007 is no tourist attraction. It is known for drugs, panhandlers and boarded-up apartments.

Despite the urban blight, the Rev. Lewis Lee has made sure this is not a God-forsaken place. Lee visits the area at least once a week to share the Gospel on the streets. He knows some of the drug dealers by name. When I found out about his ministry—and heard how many people he has prayed with in the last few years—I asked if I could go along.

I was among six men who accompanied Lee that day, and we were a motley crew: four whites, two Nigerian immigrants and Lee, a stocky African American with a broad smile and a contagious laugh. All of us were eager to share our faith and pray for people's needs. We split up into small groups and I tagged along with Lee. He had an uncanny way of breaking the ice when we approached strangers.

"Hey, how y'all doin'?" he asked three people sitting on the steps in front of an apartment building. "This is Pastor Lee, and I'm Reverend Lee. He's my brother from another mother."

We all laughed and Lee began his familiar spiel. "I need to ask you a question," he told a man who was holding a cigarette in one hand and a liquor bottle in the other. "If something happened to you, God forbid, where would you spend eternity?"

We asked that blunt question of about thirty people that afternoon—including an 83-year-old woman named Ms. Irene who was not sure of her salvation even though she said she attended church. We led her in a sinner's prayer while we stood at the intersection of Monument Street and Collington Avenue.

We prayed with all kinds of people on the sidewalks. A man named Lesley admitted he had an addiction and asked for God's help to break it. A woman asked if Lee's church could give her a ride to services on Sunday. A young Asian man named David admitted he was a backslider and listened as I shared the story of God's unconditional love for prodigals.

A beggar with crippled feet told me he knew he needed salvation. I put my arm around him while we prayed the sinner's prayer together on the steps where he begs for spare change every day. Then a woman we had prayed with fifteen minutes earlier walked by and offered to take the beggar to church with her.

Most of the people we talked to were friendly and receptive—except for two angry men who said they had no use for Jesus because they followed an Afrocentric religion. One drunken man who prayed with my friends Danny and Brandon was instantly sobered and abandoned his twelve-pack of beer on the street. By the time our team reconvened in a parking lot, at least a dozen people had given their hearts to the Lord.

Lee has been sharing the Gospel in this needy neighborhood for almost two years, and he also takes teams from his church, Evangel Cathedral, to malls and bus stops in suburban areas of the city. In that brief time, he has recorded more than 23,000 decisions—but his mission is not about collecting names for a report. He simply believes in a literal interpretation of Luke 14:23, which commands us to "go out into the highways and along the hedges, and compel them to come in."

I asked Lee his opinion about why many Christians aren't involved in personal evangelism. He offered three reasons:

1. **Fear.** Many simply have never shared their faith or don't know how to open a conversation about it. Others don't like to be rejected.
2. **Lack of training.** Many Christians assume they don't have the knowledge to answer tough questions. Others are not sure about their own salvation. "How can they lead someone to Christ if they really don't know if they are saved?" Lee asks.
3. **Apathy.** Says Lee: "Many Christians just come to church to be fed. The spiritual needs of other people don't affect them."

Although I've been involved in street ministry before and was active in personal evangelism as a college student, I'll admit it had been a long time since I intentionally went into any kind of neighborhood—rich, poor or middle-class—

to witness for Christ. And even though I frequently go on ministry trips to foreign countries, I realized during my time with Lewis Lee that I was shirking the Great Commission by avoiding sharing my faith in my own backyard.

After only a few hours with my brother Lewis Lee, I was convicted again that soul-winning should be a lifestyle. I also realized that evangelism has become a missing dimension in much of the modern charismatic/Pentecostal movement.

Enough of the Fluff

My friend Sujo John is a 9/11 survivor. Until I heard about his experience, the World Trade Center attack was just an event I had watched on television with the rest of the world. But when he told me about his narrow escape from the North Tower, and how he led victims of the disaster to Jesus before they died, I realized how God's mercy was at work during the collapse of all that melted steel and crushed concrete.

On that dark day, God plucked this young Indian immigrant out of the flames and commissioned him to be an evangelist. I believe Sujo's story carries a profound message for us all.

Sujo had been pursuing the American dream of wealth and success, but when the world came crashing down around him on 9/11 he made a major life adjustment. Everything changed when he heard the screams of dying people. Suddenly, in the light of eternity, his materialistic goals seemed pitifully shallow. Amid the coughing, the sirens, the unanswered cell phones and the mangled bodies, he pledged to spend the rest of his life reaching people who don't know Christ. We all need to make that decision.

I wish I could say that 9/11 woke up America. It is true that church attendance spiked for a few weeks after the tragedy. But it didn't take long for us to go back to business as usual. After the 9/11 wake-up call sounded, we began to act as arrogant and distracted as ever—in spite of the worst economic recession in decades.

The saddest part is that God's people did not learn the lesson of 9/11. Most of our churches today are still lukewarm and anemic. Our testimony is tarnished because of moral failures among our leaders. Our Gospel has been cheapened: We have abandoned the message of the cross and replaced it with the tasteless pabulum of pep talks and motivational seminars. We focus on what is marketable to the masses, and how we can cash in now on God's blessings while around us people perish.

The urgency of evangelism has become a foreign concept. Will it take another 9/11 to jolt us into reality?

More than one hundred years ago British revivalist Charles Spurgeon sounded an alarm to an apathetic church in his country. He declared that the chief object of glorifying God was winning souls. His cry was fervent: "We must see souls born unto God. If we do not, our cry should be that of Rachel: 'Give me children, or I die.'"[4]

I am sorry that is not the burden of the American church. Instead, we are busy with so much trifling. We must reclaim our core message out of the fire, like my friend Sujo did on 9/11. Perhaps we need to be reminded of the basics of the Gospel.

Human beings are sinners. The total depravity of man is not a popular doctrine in this selfish age. Tolerance has become the supreme virtue. But people have to be convinced they are filthy before they can see the need for a Savior to wash them clean. Spurgeon wrote: "To prophesy smooth things, and to extenuate the evil of our lost estate, is not the way to lead men to Jesus."

God is just, and He judges sin. When was the last time you heard a sermon about eternal punishment? The soft-sell approach has become the norm. We dare not offend anybody, especially by mentioning that hell is a real place. And we rob the Gospel of its power by removing the threat of punishment.

God's love is revealed in Jesus. It was the essence of love for the Father to send His Son to die for us. We cannot fathom the depths of that love, but we must try to convey it to a love-starved world.

Jesus provided full atonement. Many people don't respond to our appeals for salvation because we don't fully explain what Jesus did on the cross. We have to make it clear! Salvation is available because Christ did all the work of redemption and said, "It is finished." We can't earn forgiveness, but by simply trusting in His finished work we can receive it freely.

Please ask God to give you a love for lost souls. Allow the Holy Spirit to refine you and your presentation of His Gospel. We must stop preaching fluff and reclaim the true Gospel.

The Lord longs to have a people who will surrender their agendas, their comfort, their fears and their reputations in order to become His mouthpieces—like my bold, brave friends Kelechi, Jeet, Otoniel, Jeyasingh, Xuan and Lewis. I challenge you today to reclaim the ministry of evangelism. Ask Him for a fresh touch of His fire. Receive His holy boldness—and then put the trumpet to your mouth.

Questions for Discussion

1. Who do you admire as an example of courage and boldness? Why?
2. Recount a time when you shared your faith with another person. What challenges did you face? What was the outcome?
3. What is the biggest obstacle that hinders you from sharing your faith with others?
4. What do you think is the Holy Spirit's role in evangelism?
5. How would you evaluate your ability to share the plan of salvation with someone in a way that they can fully understand it?

For this is the will of God, your sanctification; that is, that you abstain from sexual immorality. . . . For God has not called us for the purpose of impurity, but in sanctification. So, he who rejects this is not rejecting man but the God who gives His Holy Spirit to you.

1 Thessalonians 4:3, 7–8

We grieve [the Holy Spirit] even more if we indulge in outward acts of sin. Then he is sometimes so grieved that he takes his flight for a season, for the dove will not dwell in our hearts if we take loathsome carrion in there. The dove is a clean being, and we must not strew the place which the dove frequents with filth and mire; if we do he will fly elsewhere. If we commit sin, if we openly bring disgrace on our religion, if we tempt others to sin by our example, it is not long before the Holy Spirit will begin to grieve.

Charles Spurgeon, British preacher (1834–1892)[1]

4

The Fire of Purity

I will never forget the day in November 2006 when I heard the news about Colorado pastor Ted Haggard's affair with a gay man. I was ministering in Brisbane, Australia. As soon as the scandal broke, it was all over television even on the other side of the world. In some reports, glib newscasters seemed pleased that one of the leaders of the worldwide evangelical movement couldn't control his sexual appetite. Others seemed eager to use Ted's moral failure as proof that Christians shouldn't expect homosexuals to change their sexual behavior.

Ted's fall from grace was painful for me because I had known Ted since his early days as pastor of New Life Church. His ministry style was refreshing because he was approachable and genuine. His teaching was gut-level honest as well as Bible-based. He was respected throughout the world as a leader. His seminars for pastors had grown increasingly popular.

His influence, especially in the political realm, had increased exponentially—to the point that he was included in regular White House conference calls. Noncharismatics liked him so much they elected him to lead the National Association of Evangelicals. Yet as the story of his fall from grace unfolded, we all realized that Ted had been living a double life. On the surface he was a happy family man. Underneath, he was tormented by dark addictions.

Haggard admitted that while he was pastoring his megachurch he would periodically drive an hour north to Denver to rendezvous with a male prostitute. How could this be? When I first heard the story on the radio in Australia, I was sure it was some kind of false accusation—probably concocted by a person who wanted to stop Ted's political activism. But then I heard Ted's familiar voice on the news. It was a sound byte from a recording taken from the male prostitute's telephone voicemail. My heart sank when I realized this nightmare was true.

One of my heroes had fallen.

I had to battle anger, disappointment and a huge sense of betrayal. (I can't begin to fathom what his closest associates at New Life Church endured.) I didn't know Ted struggled with homosexual feelings (he later explained that he had battled this since a childhood experience), and I didn't know he was capable of hurting his wife and family this way. When I interviewed him in July 2009, more than two years after his fall, he explained in a nutshell how he came to make such a huge mistake, and what he had learned since:

> I learned that what I had been teaching others for years is true: We should all live our lives as though there is no such thing as a secret. And I realize how much my sin costs others. Secrecy empowers sin. What I should have done is find a safe place to openly confess my sin and find a path to effective repentance. I am deeply sorry for those I have hurt and disappointed in my process.[2]

Fortunately, in Ted's case, his marriage was salvaged—thanks to his wife Gayle's amazing level of forgiveness. But

Ted's fall exposed a huge crack in the walls of our movement. Along with several other high-profile moral failures in our ranks in recent years, the Haggard scandal revealed just how deep sexual sin has seeped into a church that claims to walk in the power of the Holy Spirit. The truth is that this current generation of church leadership has rendered itself powerless when facing the Goliath of sexual compromise.

Jezebel in God's House

I wish I could say that moral failure is a sad exception in our movement. But in recent years it has become so common among charismatic leaders that some people cynically associate Pentecostal or charismatic churches with sexual sin.

Possibly the worst example of this moral backsliding involved Bishop Earl Paulk, founder of the Cathedral of the Holy Spirit in suburban Atlanta. A dynamic communicator with roots in the Church of God (Cleveland, Tennessee), Paulk built a huge congregation and an impressive ten thousand-seat Gothic sanctuary. In the early 1980s he was viewed as an innovator in creative ministry, and his church was honored by President George H. W. Bush as a "Point of Light" because of its outreach to the community.

But something was rotten at the core of Paulk's cathedral. In the early 1990s, a group of women went public with accusations that they had been coerced into sexual relationships with male staff members at the church. One had been involved sexually with Paulk's brother, a staff pastor. Another woman claimed to have had an affair with Earl. Others claimed to have been sexually harassed by a youth pastor who was related to Earl.

Many parishioners walked out when it became known that Paulk had encouraged his top-tier leaders to engage in wife-swapping. A few years later the church paid an undisclosed financial settlement to a young woman who said she had been involved sexually with Earl Paulk when she was underage.

The church's leadership had become a demonic nest of unspeakable immorality. And this was a church that regularly taught about the baptism of the Holy Spirit and offered a weekly class called "Life and Growth in the Spirit."

Paulk, who died in 2009, reportedly taught his closest followers that men who had achieved a certain level of authority in the Kingdom of God were permitted to have sex with women other than their wives. The pastor created a bizarre cult of secrecy to cover his immorality, which included an affair with his sister-in-law. That immoral union resulted in the birth of Donnie Earl Paulk, who grew up in the church thinking he was Earl's nephew until 2008 when his mother told the truth.

Today, Donnie Earl serves as pastor of what remains of the Cathedral of the Holy Spirit's dwindling congregation. The grand, Gothic building—once admired as a charismatic showcase—was sold. Donnie Earl went on to embrace full-blown heresy. He now teaches that all people, not just Christians, are saved. He told *Charisma* that the Cathedral "has expanded to include all of God's creation—Christian, Jew, Hindu, Buddhist, gay, straight, etc." This message is broadcast from a pulpit that once hosted the premier leaders of the charismatic movement.[3]

Was it supposed to end this way? How did such an influential charismatic body that was at one time focused on winning people to Christ and introducing them to the power of the Holy Spirit end in such disgrace?

I hear the sound of bricks and steel beams crashing to the ground. The wrecking ball of heaven is swinging. It has come to demolish any work that has not been built on the integrity of God's Word. You cannot build a ministry with the wood, hay and stubble of immorality and sexual sin.

All of us should be trembling. The collapse of the Cathedral of the Holy Spirit was a warning. God requires holiness in His house and truth in the mouths of His servants. He is loving and patient with our mistakes and weaknesses, but eventually, if there is no repentance after continued correction, His discipline is severe. He will not be mocked. Romans 11:22 says: "Behold then the kindness and severity of God; to those who fell, severity, but to you, God's kindness, if you continue in His kindness; otherwise you also will be cut off."

God is not married to our ministries, our television studios or our cathedrals. If He allowed foreign armies to burn Jerusalem and destroy its glorious Temple, He will also write "Ichabod" on the doors of churches where there is no repentance for sexual compromise. I pray the fear of God will grip our hearts until we cleanse our defiled pulpits.

Strange Fire on Defiled Altars

We don't talk much today about Nadab and Abihu. They were obscure Bible characters who failed miserably. Certainly their tragic story doesn't work well as an illustration in the typical seeker-friendly sermon about wealth or success. So we tend to ignore these men, even though they are mentioned in the Old Testament nine times.

Both sons of Aaron the priest, Nadab and Abihu were suddenly struck dead in the Tabernacle because they offered "strange fire" (Leviticus 10:1). We aren't told exactly what they did wrong—that is left to our imagination. All we know is that they did not follow God's specific instructions when offering incense. They were careless with His glory. Their mistake proved to be fatal.

Something we clearly deduce from their story is that God's altar is a holy place. When God struck them, He told their father: "By those who come near Me I will be treated as holy, and before all the people I will be honored" (verse 3). God made it clear that He isn't playing games. He sent fire from His presence to slay Nadab and Abihu so we would understand that we are not to mess around with His laws, His name or His presence. We can't rewrite His instructions or be slipshod or slapdash about worship.

That's why I fear for many of the men and women who claim to be God's mouthpieces today, particularly when they seem to be so cavalier about sexual morality. When I read Leviticus 10, I wonder why the ground has not opened up and swallowed some of the careless playboys who are masquerading as bishops, apostles and prophets today.

A case in point: Bishop Thomas Wesley Weeks III, who stood in his pulpit in Atlanta during a marriage conference in 2007 and taught married couples how to use profanity during sex. He told attendees at a "Teach Me How to Love You" event that they should get over their hang-ups about profanity. The bedroom, he said, is the place to get down and dirty.

"Don't bring your salvation into the bedroom," Weeks said in a sermon segment that was posted on the internet. "All those special words that you can't say no more because you're saved . . . save that for the bedroom!"[4]

It is bad enough that Weeks told his followers that it's acceptable to use filthy language with our spouses during lovemaking. It's worse that he said these things during a church service. He has taken pulpit crudity to a new level, and because his example goes unchallenged, someone else is sure to espouse Pentecostal porn to an audience somewhere. In fact, it has happened. When I was in Holland a few years ago, I learned that a charismatic minister was teaching that apostles are permitted to have more than one wife. After spreading this doctrine to his followers on three continents, he left his wife and married a much younger woman.

Weeks's comments didn't surprise me. There are so many crazy things happening in pulpits in this country that I've become numb to their impact. It seems that in many segments of the Church today, false prophets and backslidden preachers can introduce the most bizarre doctrines imaginable and still get shouts from the crowd and plenty of donations in the offering plate. Consider:

- In one city on the East Coast, a flamboyant Pentecostal preacher with a large church and huge television audience found himself in the midst of scandal. The local newspaper had reported that he had fathered several children out of wedlock and that his wife was leaving him because of it. Rather than apologize for his mistakes, the pastor preached a sermon about how God forgave King David for his adultery. He then declared, "I'm still the man!" and his congregation rallied behind him. His "I'm Still the Man!" sermon became popular in some church circles.

- In the Southeast, a charismatic preacher who is regularly seen hosting a Christian television program was caught in an adulterous affair. He had been seeing a woman he met in a strip club in Europe, and his wife filed for divorce when she found out about his unfaithfulness. The pastor never told his congregation what he did, and he continued preaching from the pulpit and from the national television platform. He showed no remorse for his actions.

I have no personal vendetta against these people, but I have no problem saying they are the modern counterparts of Nadab and Abihu. They are spiritual hoodlums. They are playing with strange fire. They have no business remaining in ministry, and they will answer to God for the damage they have caused.

Lately I find myself praying: "Lord, when will You clean up Your Church? When will You send Your holy fire into the sanctuary? When will You turn over the tables of the money-changers and drive the charlatans out of Your house?"

I have a sense the answer is coming soon enough.

A Fuzzy-Wuzzy Morality

It seems that in many of our churches today, up is down, right is wrong and biblical absolutes are up for grabs. This is especially true when it comes to marriage, an institution that once was considered sacred. Nowadays, many preachers and even famous evangelical authors have created a new trend: throwaway wedding vows. Christian divorce today is cheap and easy. Some of our superstar preachers have even figured out a way to use Bible verses to support their moral failures.

In 2007 a prominent charismatic ministry couple announced they were divorcing. Randy and Paula White, founders of Without Walls Church in Tampa, Florida, gave no clear explanation why they were splitting up. The Whites said adultery was not the reason for their breakup, although Randy said the whole mess was his fault. We were all left scratching our heads.

Paula continued on her whirlwind ministry circuit without skipping a beat, teaching people how to live "a life by design," the official name of her trademark success seminars. But I was left questioning what kind of design she and Randy were promoting—especially when she joined the staff of a church in Texas led by a pastor who had divorced his wife a year earlier. By partnering with him in ministry, Paula seemed to be legitimizing the other pastor's divorce.

When a local television reporter in Tampa asked Paula about how she reconciles her faith with her decision to divorce, she quoted a verse from Ecclesiastes. She implied that, just as there is "a time for everything under heaven," her divorce was merely an unfortunate moment in her spiritual journey. She also suggested that one day she and Randy might get back together since they are good friends.

What garbled message did this send to immature believers who don't know yet how to discern God's will for themselves? Many of them will take Paula's confusing words as license

88

to do whatever is right in their own eyes. If there is a "time for divorce," then what else can we justify that there is "a time for"? Binge drinking? A porn movie? Stealing from an employer? I wish Paula had said this: "Divorce is not God's will. It destroys families. It's why Jesus said what He did about it. If anyone out there is thinking about divorce, please don't choose that path until you have tried every avenue for restoration." But she didn't sound a clear trumpet, as a minister of God is called to do. Instead, she offered mishmash.

Then we have the case of Bishop Thomas Wesley Weeks III, who I mentioned earlier in this chapter as the minister who encouraged profanity in the bedroom. Weeks and his celebrated wife, Pentecostal preacher Juanita Bynum, had their million-dollar wedding ceremony aired on Christian television in 2004. But their marriage crashed and burned three years later when Bynum accused Weeks of beating her in an Atlanta hotel parking lot. Both continued preaching after their divorce. There was no talk of stepping down for a time of restoration. In fact, Weeks immediately began talking to the media about what kind of wife he wanted to replace Bynum.

What was missing in both the Weeks-Bynum fiasco and the Whites' breakup was a clear admission that biblical principles had been violated. For the Whites, we were left feeling that if a couple drifts apart because of the demands of ministry, the correct response is to just move on and keep preaching. For Bynum and Weeks, the message was also muddled: If your marriage doesn't work out, it's probably because your partner didn't realize how powerful God's calling is on your life. (In other words, it's all about you.)

This sad scenario seems almost normal today because our standards have been badly compromised. In many independent charismatic churches we refuse to draw any boundaries. We don't enforce biblical standards of leadership. We don't tell those who have failed morally to get out of the ministry long enough to find true healing. Could this be the main reason why the divorce rate among Christians continues to mirror that of the general population?

The Scandal of Greasy Grace

This tragic lack of a moral compass was most obvious after the embarrassing moral failure involving Canadian evangelist Todd Bentley, leader of what became known as the Lakeland Revival in Florida. That four-month period of nightly meetings ended abruptly in 2008 after it became known that Bentley had decided to leave his wife and marry a younger woman who had served him as a ministry intern.

Thankfully, the governing board of Bentley's Fresh Fire Ministries in British Columbia publicly scolded him for committing adultery. But in a subsequent statement released by charismatic author Rick Joyner, who was overseeing Bentley's restoration process, we were told that Bentley planned to relaunch his ministry, called Fresh Fire USA, near Charlotte, North Carolina. Joyner said he was collecting donations from supporters to help rebuild it.

What was most deplorable about the Bentley scandal was the lack of true remorse. Bentley hurriedly remarried immediately after his divorce was final. Before the ink was dry on that document, people were clamoring to have this man back in the pulpit. It revealed a fundamental weakness in our approach toward sin.

This is all contrary to New Testament faith. When the apostle Paul learned that a member of the Corinthian church was in an immoral relationship with the man's father's wife, he did not rush to comfort the man. Nor did he downplay the sin, tiptoe around the scandal or redefine morality in light of the popular moral climate.

He told the Corinthians: "You have become arrogant and have not mourned instead, so that the one who had done this deed would be removed from your midst" (1 Corinthians 5:2).

Paul drew a ruthless sword in order to bring genuine healing. The "wounds of a friend" are faithful to bring conviction and true repentance (Proverbs 27:6).

Paul actually delivered the unrepentant Corinthian man to Satan "for the destruction of his flesh" (1 Corinthians 5:5) so that he could be saved. That does not sound very nice. Many today would call Paul's tactic harsh and legalistic. But that is because we have lost any true sense of the fear of the Lord—and we don't realize that our laxness about God's standards is a perversion of His mercy. When the sin is severe, the public rebuke must be severe.

In all the discussion about Bentley and the demise of the Lakeland Revival, I was waiting to hear the sound of sackcloth ripping into shreds. We should have been weeping over this travesty. We should have been rending our hearts—as God commanded Israel to do when they fell into sin (Joel 2:13). To give guidance to a confused church, our leaders should have publicly decried the Lakeland disaster while at the same time helping both Bentley and his ex-wife to heal.

But there was no public mourning. Bentley's fans did not seem shocked or appalled that such sin had occurred among us. They acted as if flippant divorce and remarriage are minor infractions—when in actuality they are such serious moral failures that they can bring disqualification.

If we truly loved Todd Bentley and other fallen ministers, we would not clamor for their quick return to the pulpit. While we certainly want them to be fully restored to fellowship with God, we should never rush the process of restoring a man or woman to ministry. Leaders must live up to a higher standard. We must demand that those involved in a minister's restoration not only love him but also love the Church by protecting it from his premature return to leadership.

We need a fresh baptism of purity!

Our moral compass has been tampered with and needs to be reset according to God's Word. It is time for some back-bone. All who believe the Bible is the rulebook for marriage, sexuality, moral character and church discipline must confront this sinful handling of God's Word. We must lovingly but firmly redraw the lines before they are blurred beyond distinction.

I recommend we take these steps to recover what we've lost:

1. Address sexual sin openly. We cannot avoid this topic just because a few older people in the crowd might feel uncomfortable. In previous generations it was considered unseemly to talk about sex in a church service. But today we cannot afford to be prudish. The Bible is not rated G. We are in a spiritual war. Satan is using sex as a weapon to destroy lives, and we have to confront things head-on.

This is especially true as we address the younger generation. Today's young people are being bombarded with confusion and compromise when it comes to sexuality. They were children when President Clinton had an affair with Monica Lewinsky, and they've seen and heard it all thanks to easy access to internet porn, crude Hollywood films and pop music lyrics. But they rarely hear Christian leaders speaking honestly about how God feels about sexual sin.

I love speaking to college students on this topic. Some Christian young people roll their eyes when I say the word "fornication" because it sounds so much like King James English—sort of like "sodomy," another old-fashioned word we avoid in our PC culture. But we need to be careful how we bend the meaning of words. Terms that are in the Bible should not vanish from our modern vocabulary just because they offend. "Fornication" is actually an important Bible word we need to recover in this hour of soft morality.

First Thessalonians 4:3 says: "For this is the will of God... that ye should abstain from *fornication*" (KJV, emphasis added). The Greek word used here, *porneia*, is the root word for pornography, but it means a lot more than sexually explicit material. It includes sex between unmarried people, homosexuality, bestiality, prostitution, incest and adultery.

All fornication is off-limits. According to the apostle Paul, sex as God intended it is limited to marriage between one man and one woman. Period. The Episcopal Church had no right to broaden the definition when its leaders voted to ordain practicing homosexual clergy. Bishop Earl Paulk had no right to invent a new doctrine that allowed pastors to swap wives. And we have no right to tell people in our churches that cohabitation between two unmarried people is excusable.

In an era when our culture is waffling on every moral issue, the Church must stand up in the power of the Spirit and preach the Word without apologizing for any of it.

2. Preach abstinence. Losing one's virginity used to be a serious issue, but today fornication is nothing more than a standard sitcom plot device. It's considered normal. People are considered weird if they don't have sex by age fourteen; and if anybody dares to teach abstinence in a public school he is labeled a Neanderthal.

In television shows like *Desperate Housewives* or *Nip/Tuck*, life revolves around who's in bed with whom. There's even a TV series on Showtime called *Californication* that follows the life of a sex addict. What TV producers don't usually explore are the consequences of immorality. Audiences probably wouldn't laugh if the couples hooking up on these shows had to deal with genital warts, gonorrhea, AIDS, abortions, post-abortion trauma or clinical depression—all real fallout from illicit sexual behavior.

The world also hates the term "abstinence." Teaching sexual abstinence in schools is anathema. It is more politically correct to distribute condoms than to urge teenagers to avoid sex altogether. We can't allow this spirit of compromise to infect the Church. We must challenge single people—whether they have already lost their virginity or not—to reclaim purity and save sex for marriage.

3. Get ruthless with your weaknesses. Jesus sounded stricter than a school principal when He talked to His disciples about self-discipline. He told them: "If your right eye makes you stumble, tear it out and throw it from you; for it is better for you to lose one of the parts of your body, than for your whole body to be thrown into hell" (Matthew 5:29).

Jesus was not advocating self-mutilation. He was using sarcasm to emphasize how serious sin is—and He urged His followers to take radical steps to avoid the snares of temptation. In our sex-soaked society, it is more imperative than ever that we draw boundaries.

Do you have a problem with pornography? If you can't discipline yourself to avoid offending websites, get rid of your computer. Do you end up engaging in heavy petting or intercourse with your girlfriend or boyfriend after a few minutes of kissing? Draw lines and stick to them. And if you can't stick to the rules, ask for intervention. If you don't, you are headed for spiritual shipwreck.

4. Live a transparent life. The Bible never advocates that we battle sin alone. We need each other. James 5:16 says: "Therefore, confess your sins to one another, and pray for one another so that you may be healed." In some cases you will never get victory over temptation until you share your struggle with a trusted Christian friend or mentor and seek counsel and prayer.

So many believers today live with secrets. Many women (and men too) were molested as children by relatives or friends—yet they have never shared their pain. Many young men are trapped in a dark world of pornography and masturbation but are too ashamed to admit it. Many Christians struggle with same-sex attraction yet they fear that if they confess their thoughts they will be rejected.

You will never discover the abundant life Christ promised until you clean out your spiritual closets and deal with all your dirty laundry. Total forgiveness and cleansing are available, but confession and repentance must come first.

5. Develop the fear of God. Paul had sober words for the Thessalonians who ignored his admonitions about sexual sin. He told them: "He who rejects this is not rejecting man but the God who gives His Holy Spirit to you" (1 Thessalonians 4:8). It couldn't be clearer: If you disregard sexual boundaries, you are on thin ice.

What we desperately need in the Church today is a conscience awakening. Too many Christians have warped judgment—and they don't even feel godly remorse when they break God's law. If you have any form of sexual sin in your life, flee it immediately and make a 180-degree turn. He will grant you the grace to live a life of purity.

6. Return to biblical church discipline. Leaders must be godly examples. God does not require them to have perfect marriages, but He does raise the bar for all those called into the ministry by requiring marital faithfulness. We don't have the right to lower that bar just because we live in a permissive culture.

We must make biblical standards clear: (1) Marriage is indeed sacred, and divorce should never be viewed as a casual choice, (2) ministers of the Gospel should have exemplary marriages and (3) leaders who fail at marriage can be instantly forgiven, but they have no business leading a church until they have walked through a healing process that includes full repentance and a heavy dose of accountability.

Unfortunately, in much of our free-floating world of independent charismatic churches, there is no such thing as an enforceable standard of professional behavior. Physicians must be licensed by the state, and we would never go to a surgeon who got his medical degree from a diploma mill. But we allow ministers to be freelancers. A doctor has to obey the rules, but our preachers don't. We make up the rules as we go.

As I mentioned in a previous chapter, Paul Cain, the celebrated charismatic prophet who appeared in countless conference pulpits during the 1990s, stepped down from ministry in 2005 after he was publicly confronted for his immoral conduct. Cain admitted his failures and initially agreed to submit to a regimen of accountability prescribed by a group of men who knew him. But a few weeks later, he announced that he was moving to California to find restoration from a different group—a church that Cain's disciplinary oversight team of Mike Bickle, Rick Joyner and Jack Deere knew nothing about.

Then, twelve months later, *voila!* The church in California announced that Cain was "restored" and ready to preach again. Bickle, Joyner and Deere did the right thing by releasing a statement that said, in part: "We cannot say with confidence that this is a genuine restoration that is according to the principles of God's Word. It will be harmful to [Cain] and others if he is released prematurely and then relapses into his past failures."

Thank God someone was bold enough to demand a higher standard—at a time when so many Christians have closed their eyes to biblical morality. Cain's situation gave us an opportunity to examine our movement's credibility crisis. We need clearer guidelines on how to handle a leader's moral failure. Here are four principles we must keep in mind when dealing with sin among church leaders.

- **Forgiveness is immediate.** God's mercy is amazing, and He is quick to forgive a fallen leader who repents. God does not require us to wallow in shame or self-pity. We can eagerly embrace the redemption that Christ purchased for us.

- **Personal restoration is a process.** Repentance is not just feeling sorry for making a mistake. A leader must have heartfelt humility and a genuine sense of brokenness for the way his or her sin hurt others. If the leader is in denial about his failures, true friends must confront his deeply rooted pride and deception.

- **Restoration to ministry should never be fast-tracked.** Many experts suggest that a fallen leader should step down for a minimum of three years in order to find full healing in his own life as well as in marriage (especially in the case of sexual sin). Some denominations require only two years of rehabilitation, but those of us in independent churches have required even less time. As a result of our hurry, there are many unhealed, unhealthy leaders in the pulpit today—as well as congregations that feel exploited by spiritual traitors.

- **Restoration should involve people who know the fallen leader.** If a leader fails morally, he will be tempted to find a new community and set of friends who are wowed by his charisma but don't see his dark side. True restoration must include reconciliation with the people hurt by his actions.

It is time for a baptism of purity. We must stand with the apostle Paul, who drew unpopular lines in the sand, demanded character of church leaders and warned early Christians to avoid the self-restored Lone Rangers of that era. If we don't draw clear lines today, we'll pay in consequences we can't imagine.

Questions for Discussion

1. Give some possible reasons why you think there is an epidemic of moral failure in the Church today.
2. Nadab and Abihu offered "strange fire" on the Lord's altar (Leviticus 10:1). Name some types of strange fire being offered in churches today.
3. How can we teach people today to honor God's sexual boundaries when there is so much immorality in our culture—and in our churches?
4. How does regular confession of sin and a transparent lifestyle help us avoid sexual sin?
5. Suppose a pastor or evangelist falls into an adulterous affair. How should his church or denomination respond to this crisis?

Take particular care in picking out your building materials. Eventually there is going to be an inspection. If you use cheap or inferior materials, you'll be found out. The inspection will be thorough and rigorous. You won't get by with a thing. If your work passes inspection, fine; if it doesn't, your part of the building will be torn out and started over. But *you* won't be torn out; you'll survive—but just barely.

1 Corinthians 3:12–15, MESSAGE

How careful you should be in the great matters of morality, honesty and integrity! Here the minister must not fail. His private life must ever keep good tune with his ministry, or his day will soon set with him, and the sooner he retires the better, for his continuance in his office will only dishonor the cause of God and ruin himself.

Charles Spurgeon[1]

5

The Fire of Integrity

I play the popular praise chorus "Healer" all the time in my car. I can't get the tune out of my head. You may know the words:

> I believe You're my healer
> I believe You are all I need
> I believe You're my portion
> I believe You're more than enough for me
> Jesus You're all I need.[2]

Thousands of churches have been singing the popular worship chorus since Australian youth pastor Michael Guglielmucci wrote it in 2008. The Aussie worship band Hillsong United has made it a global anthem, and it's especially popular among people battling illness. But the song took on a darker meaning when Guglielmucci admitted it was part of an elaborate hoax he created.

Christians around the world felt shocked and betrayed when the young minister admitted he had faked cancer for two years in a strange ploy to hide his secret pornography addiction. The fiasco became one of the biggest scandals to rock Australia's Christian community.

In a tearful apology aired on Australian television, Guglielmucci said he faked symptoms and wrote bogus emails from doctors. He sat in waiting rooms alone while his family assumed he was getting treatment. He appeared in church concerts with an oxygen tube in his nose, deceiving thousands of mostly teenage fans into believing he needed a physical healing.

This talented but tormented young man eventually trapped himself in his own deceptive web. Church leaders asked him to confess his lies to the police, since he used the story to raise funds. He was stripped of his ministerial credentials and enrolled in a program offering psychiatric help. Australian church leaders, including pastor Brian Houston of Hillsong Church in Sydney, had to make public statements to calm distraught churchgoers who felt betrayed and, in some cases, were defrauded of their money.

I can't begin to imagine the pain that Guglielmucci's parents feel. (His father is a pastor who read his son's apology to a stunned congregation outside Adelaide.) I am sure trust was severely damaged among members of Guglielmucci's family. But how do we respond when a leader fails us like this?

Thankfully, in Guglielmucci's case, he did not justify his behavior. His apology was read in churches all over Australia. He told a news reporter: "I'm so sorry not just for lying to my friends and family even about a sickness, but I'm sorry for a life of saying I was something when I'm not. From this day on I'm telling the truth."[3]

This sad drama from Down Under reveals a global problem that the Church must face. It goes much deeper than a porn addiction. It reveals a fundamental lack of integrity. It is the reason we face a serious leadership crisis in today's Church.

Sound the Alarm

Louisiana pastor Larry Stockstill had a disturbing dream one night in 2008. He saw military trucks and armored vehicles

100

getting information for a surprise strike on an American city. In the dream Stockstill was alarmed by what he saw, but when he tried to warn a pastor the man ignored him.

"In my dream I knew that a siege was going to happen the next day," Stockstill told me. "The enemy was being positioned. But no one would listen to me."

Stockstill, pastor of the ten thousand-member Bethany World Prayer Center in Baton Rouge, believes his dream was a prophetic warning about the spiritual condition of our nation. While America is teetering near an economic and political precipice, many American church leaders are going on with their business as usual—without realizing that the church is in a state of serious moral crisis.

"I believe we are facing a window of opportunity for repentance," Stockstill said. "Unless the pastors wake up to avert judgment, there will be judgment on America. If we don't respond we are going to lose this nation."

Stockstill became alarmed about the anemic condition of American churches in 2006, when he had to step in and help oversee the disciplining of Ted Haggard, the Colorado Springs pastor who was removed as senior leader of New Life Church because of a moral failure. Stockstill offered correction and oversight to Haggard and his family and helped the leaders of New Life pick up the pieces after the scandal. Many observers praised Stockstill for his level-headed leadership and compassionate but strict adherence to biblical principles during the crisis.

What Stockstill learned during that painful process became the basis of a book, *The Remnant: Restoring Integrity to American Ministry*. In it he writes these painful words:

> It is amazing to me that as our churches grow larger, our nation grows seemingly darker morally. The church seems obsessed with growth and "relating" to America, but it reminds me of Samson before his haircut. Though engaged in immorality, Samson continued to function in his gift for years.

How can an individual continue to grow a huge church or ministry and yet be struggling with secret sin? The answer is simple: A person's gift will make room for him and attract the notice and attention of others. Furthermore, that gift, though legitimate and God given, can be operated in pride and arrogance rather than in submission to God.[4]

Stockstill, who has avoided the national spotlight during most of his 33 years in ministry, also told me in the interview: "We look like a sleaze bucket in the eyes of the nation." Once a missionary in Africa, Stockstill has focused most of his ministry on church planting and missions. Bethany has helped start more than seventeen thousand churches worldwide since 2000.

Stockstill says the level of dysfunction among American ministers concerns him because their unhealthiness is then passed down to their congregations. He sees five types of common dysfunction among ministers today, especially in the independent charismatic movement:

- **Lack of fathering** (no affirmation, encouragement or spiritual covering).
- **Lack of correction** (no accountability, resulting in pride and moral failure).
- **Lack of fruitfulness** (no training in evangelism and discipleship, preventing churches from multiplying as they should).
- **Lack of healing** (many pastors suffer silently because of sins and addictions).
- **Lack of teaching** (many in ministry today are untaught, resulting in biblically illiterate churches).

You might notice that each of these five areas of lack corresponds to the five essential ministries Jesus gave to the Church, as listed in Ephesians 4:11–12: apostle, prophet, evangelist, pastor and teacher. Apostles provide foundations and spiritual covering; prophets bring correction; evangelists equip churches to be fruitful in reaching the lost; pastors bring healing; and teachers train churches in the Word of God.

Essentially what the Church is facing in this hour is a serious leadership crisis. And Stockstill does not believe we have very much time to fix the problem. "We really have to relay the foundations of ministry in this country," he told me in a 2008 interview. "Many pastors have not been fathered, so they become 'posers'—they are just looking to impress people."

Pride, Stockstill says, is a primary reason why so many leaders in the American church have fallen in recent years—including mature spiritual fathers who had years of successful ministry behind them but stumbled in their later years. "You look at leaders in the Bible like Solomon, or like Samson, and you find that years of success can lead a person into pride. And when pride comes, it brings a lack of accountability."

Where Have All the Leaders Gone?

The people of Israel faced a leadership crisis during their sojourn in the wilderness. From morning until evening, dozens of people would line up outside Moses' tent to ask him to resolve a dispute. When his father-in-law, Jethro, saw the crowds outside his door, he pulled Moses aside and gave him wise advice.

Jethro warned his son-in-law that he would burn out if he continued to govern the nation by himself. He told Moses: "You shall select out of all the people able men who fear God, men of truth, those who hate dishonest gain; and you shall place these over them as leaders of thousands, of hundreds, of fifties and of tens" (Exodus 18:21).

In the middle of the Sinai desert, Jethro taught the first management seminar. But his counsel was not just about the principle of delegation; he was also stressing the importance of godly character in leaders. In fact, he makes it clear that people who lack character should be excluded from leadership positions.

Jethro could have identified other qualities as prerequisites for leadership. He could have mentioned charisma, sex appeal, preaching ability, musical talent, intellect, organizational skills, business know-how, wealth, pedigree or high ratings in political polls. But none of those are God's requirements. Jethro mentioned three qualities that we desperately need in the church as well as in mainstream culture.

1. Leaders who fear God. A person who fears God lives in a continual attitude of reverence—whether he is alone or in front of a crowd. He is aware that God is watching his actions and weighing his words. Because this person cares more about pleasing God than people, he takes God's moral standards seriously—and he depends on the Holy Spirit to help him make right choices.

You don't have to look far to see that the American church has fallen short when it comes to the fear of God. Just turn to the previous chapter to read about the Florida preacher who carried on an affair with a stripper. If we apply the Jethro principle, this man should be out of the ministry today. The sad truth is he is still preaching—and has a crowd following him.

A person who fears God is never flippant about morality. Because he keeps his conscience clean he is immediately convicted if he makes an unkind remark, entertains a lustful thought or sets a bad example. He's also aware that if he doesn't quickly repent when he grieves the Holy Spirit, his conscience could become callous. So he regularly examines his motives, conversations, appetites and relationships to make sure he's not veering off course. God, give us leaders who fear You!

2. Leaders who tell the truth. We live in a dishonest culture. The 2007 financial crisis was triggered, in part, by people who lied when they applied for home loans. Bank executives have admitted that mortgages were granted even to people who worked service jobs and yet claimed six-figure salaries. When people who lied about their incomes couldn't pay their mortgages, they defaulted on their loans and the system imploded. The greedy financial sharks who sold those loans lied, too. Then taxpayers had to pay for the ensuing meltdown.

Our moral system will suffer a similar collapse if we don't return to truth. The Church should set the standard for integrity—and that includes honest accounting practices, full financial disclosure and an end to the "evang*elastic*" stretching of the truth that is so common in our ranks. If we realized that heaven keeps a record of "every careless word" we speak (Matthew 12:36), we would stop exaggerating our ministry reports. God, give us leaders who tell the truth!

3. Leaders who hate dishonest gain. Most of us shook our heads in disgust in 2008 when we heard about Governor Rod Blagojevich's outlandish bribery scandal. After being arrested for attempting to sell Barack Obama's Senate seat, the embattled Illinois politician dug in his heels and insisted on appointing the state attorney general to the vacant spot. Blagojevich turned the evening news into a three-ring circus.

You know it's bad when the governor of a populous state gets caught telling people that he wants a wad of money in exchange for a political appointment. It shows how deeply moral corruption has infected our system. What's worse is that this corruption is mirrored in many of our churches.

Greed has actually morphed into a virtue in some charismatic circles, where pastors take hourlong offerings and guest speakers require limousines and five-figure honorariums to maintain their celebrity lifestyles. It's especially bad on some Christian TV channels, where spiritual extortionists sell medieval-style indulgences disguised as "Day of Atonement offerings" and use other ridiculous ploys to rob Christians. God, give us leaders who hate dishonest gain!

It's time for a leadership reformation. True spiritual revival will not come to the American church until we take Jethro's counsel seriously, removing corrupt leaders from their positions and replacing them with those who match the biblical standard. But how can we begin to enact this kind of godly discipline?

Cowardice, Compromise and the Sin of Eli

No biblical character is more pitiful than Eli, the Levite priest who compromised his ministry and defiled God's house because he couldn't bring himself to discipline his two wayward sons. The Bible says Hophni and Phinehas were "worthless men" (1 Samuel 2:12). That was putting it mildly. These rascals, dressed up in sweet-smelling priestly garb, were responsible for one of the first religious sex scandals in history. They became Eli's greatest shame.

Not only did these men prey on vulnerable women (and engage in sex with them in the very doorway of the house of God), but they also were involved in the worst kind of financial exploitation. They cunningly manipulated people while taking offerings; then they misused the gifts for their own sordid gain.

Eli's fatal flaw reminds me of a problem we face today. He was timid about confronting sin. He danced around the real problems. He lived in denial—at a time when the Church was in moral crisis.

Even though Eli questioned his sons' behavior and warned them of the consequences, he did not remove them from their positions. Even though the people in the pews were shocked by Hophni and Phinehas's sexual escapades and financial shenanigans, Eli let his privileged boys go right on taking offerings and raping parishioners. Year after year he allowed his sons to mock God and infect people with their corruption.

The story does not end well. Because sin had entered the camp of God's people, the ark of God's presence was captured by the Philistines, and Hophni and Phinehas were killed in the raid. The Bible paints an ugly picture of the scene when Eli hears the news of his sons' deaths: "Eli fell off the seat backward beside the gate, and his neck was broken and he died, for he was old and heavy" (1 Samuel 4:18).

That's not a flattering obituary. Perhaps the Bible uses such graphic language, including the mention of Eli's obesity, to drive home the point that this pathetic priest was not only timid but also selfish and undisciplined in his personal life.

What does Eli have to do with us? After all, he lived in Old Testament times, right? There are plenty of charismatic leaders today who have adopted a theology of greasy grace and sloppy holiness. Their sole mantra is, "Mercy." They say there is no longer any need for church discipline or moral standards in leadership.

When I wrote an article in *Charisma* in 2008 about the need for tough new policies for restoring fallen leaders, a chorus of critics claimed I was acting like a judgmental Pharisee. More than one person declared, "All have sinned, so who are we to judge if a leader has an affair?" Others said, "If a leader is involved in some kind of sexual sin, God forgives him instantly. He can be in the pulpit the next day." Still others protested, "Leaders in the New Testament church never stepped down from their positions because of sin."

All this shows how spineless we've become. We are afraid to stand for what is right for fear of seeming intolerant or self-righteous. Among independent charismatic churches in America, we've developed a culture that retreats from genuine discipline and makes it easy for disgraced leaders to return to the pulpit without having dealt with their sin. But I don't see this lax attitude in the apostle Paul, who set high standards of character for all his leaders, blacklisted false teachers and even excommunicated people who continued in immorality.

Paul went so far as to turn certain wayward leaders over to Satan so they would learn their lesson. He rebuked false teachers by name. And his excommunication of immoral "pseudo-Christians" was to uphold biblical standards as well as to draw the sinner back to grace.

All this may sound extreme, but extreme sin requires extreme measures. Godly leaders draw lines and enforce moral standards—without becoming self-righteous and unkind. Ungodly leaders, on the other hand, may appear to be nice and compassionate, but they actually are unfaithful to God if they refuse to require their spiritual sons and daughters to follow biblical standards of behavior.

I agree with Pastor Larry Stockstill that we are in a moment of serious leadership crisis in the American church, and part of our problem is the sin of Eli. I am making an appeal: It is time for the fathers and mothers of the Church to do their job. We need their rebuke and their rod of correction. If they don't, the Hophnis and Phineases of our generation will gain the upper hand until God is forced to step in with swift judgment.

Time to Stop the Funny Business

This lack of moral backbone became obvious recently in the city of Baltimore, where a prominent pastor ended up in the newspaper because of his scandalous behavior. I mentioned this man's example in the previous chapter. Jamal Harrison-Bryant, pastor of Empowerment Temple in Baltimore, was accused of fathering a child out of wedlock. His wife, Gizelle, citing adultery and cruel treatment, filed for divorce in 2009. Yet Harrison-Bryant preached a now-famous sermon in the church in which he used King David's story of adultery with Bathsheba to defend himself.

"I'm still the man!" he shouted from the pulpit as worshipers stood and cheered. "The anointing on my life is greater than any mistake."[5] He made it clear that he had no intention of being defrocked or disciplined. To Harrison-Bryant, anointing surpasses character. Whether he had one, two or nine illegitimate children was irrelevant. What mattered was his ability to make a crowd swoon when he took the stage. He had the uncanny ability to comfort and console people about his own sins with his smooth religious words.

Harrison-Bryant's total disregard for Christian character is sad enough. What makes the situation worse is that the leaders around him did not demand he step down and get help for his problems. Harrison-Bryant was a part of the African Methodist Episcopal denomination. Yet apparently no one took action against Harrison-Bryant's sin. Like Eli, they seemed powerless to bring the needed correction.

All this moral failure among leaders today has the average Christian confused. Is there ever a time when leaders are disqualified? Is restoration always immediate? Are we acting like Pharisees if we demand that leaders sit on the bench for a while to recover from their mistakes and prove their character again? It is time for us to restate some obvious rules.

1. There are definite qualifications for Christian leadership. The apostle Paul made it clear there is a litmus test for leaders in the New Testament church. In 1 Timothy 3:2–7 he says a leader must be (1) above reproach, (2) the husband of one wife, (3) temperate (not an abuser of alcohol or other substances), (4) prudent, (5) respectable, (6) hospitable, (7) able to teach, (8) a good manager of his own family, (9) respected in the community and (10) not a new convert.

In his letter to Titus, Paul offers a similar list and adds further qualifications, including (11) not self-willed; (12) not pugnacious and (13) not fond of sordid gain.

Notice that only one of these qualifications ("able to teach") involves anointing. Paul says nothing about a leader's ability to prophesy, heal the sick, see visions, talk to angels, raise funds, sing, shout or make people fall on the floor by the anointing of the Holy Spirit. Nor does he mention academic credentials. Character is the key.

Many scholars agree that "husband of one wife" was a New Testament–era way of saying "he must be a one-woman

man." In other words, he cannot be an adulterer. He cannot have a girlfriend on the side. (Not to mention, he can't be polygamous.) Leaders must walk in sexual purity. They must adhere to the biblical definition of marriage and stay faithful in that context.

2. Those who do not meet these qualifications must step down. If Paul demanded character of his leaders, it stands to reason that those who fail in any of these areas should be removed from office—at least until they regain character quality after a time of rehabilitation. When leaders failed, Paul also recommended that they be strongly rebuked "in the presence of all, so that the rest also will be fearful of sinning" (1 Timothy 5:20). Their sin was never to be minimized, excused or swept under a rug.

This strict approach was not optional—and Paul warned Timothy about the temptation to be partial. He told him: "I solemnly charge you . . . to maintain these principles without bias" (verse 21). Biblical discipline cannot be sloppy. We can't remove one man for adultery and then offer kid-glove treatment to another just because he is our friend. As painful as it is to remove a gifted leader from his position, it must be done to preserve biblical morality in the fear of the Lord.

3. The church will not thrive if discipline of leaders is neglected. Paul sternly warned Timothy about ordaining any church leader prematurely. He wrote: "Do not lay hands upon anyone too hastily and thereby share responsibility for the sins of others" (1 Timothy 5:22). In other words, leaders actually incur a strict judgment from God if they ordain a leader who does not meet biblical qualifications. If ordaining unapproved leaders becomes a habit, corruption will take root in the Church and we will eventually face God's corrective judgment.

The Corinthian church was warned that the deceitfulness of sin would infect them all if they did not deal with the immorality in their midst (1 Corinthians 5:7–13). John told the church in Thyatira they would lose their influence because they tolerated false teaching that led to immorality (Revelation 2:19–20). Sin has sobering consequences.

We can't rewrite the rules. And we can't bypass the consequences, no matter how long they may be delayed. I pray that leaders in the independent sector of the church today will stop all this funny business and restore biblical order.

Questions for Discussion

1. What evidence do you see of a leadership crisis when you look at politics, local government, the business world—and the church?
2. What three character qualities did Jethro tell Moses to look for in a leader?
3. What should Eli have done when he found out how his sons were misrepresenting God as priests?
4. Read the qualities of a church overseer listed in 1 Timothy 3:2–7. Which of these qualities do you think need to be emphasized more clearly in today's Church?

Even though we had some standing as Christ's apostles, we never threw our weight around or tried to come across as important, with you or anyone else. We weren't aloof with you. We took you just as you were. We were never patronizing, never condescending, but we cared for you the way a mother cares for her children. We loved you dearly. Not content to just pass on the Message, we wanted to give you our hearts. And we did.

1 Thessalonians 2:6–8, MESSAGE

People all over the land have heard that the oil of the Spirit is being poured out in Los Angeles, and they are coming for oil—coming thousands of miles. And they are being filled with the holy oil, the baptism of the Holy Ghost, and wherever they go, it is being poured out. . . . We must give God all the glory in this work. We must keep very humble at His feet. He recognizes no flesh, no color, no names. We must not glory in Azusa Mission, nor in anything but the Lord Jesus Christ by whom the world is crucified unto us and we unto the world.

From *The Apostolic Faith* newspaper, recording the events of the Azusa Street Revival, January 1907.[1]

The way to be very great is to be very little. To be very noteworthy in your own esteem is to be unnoticed of God. If you must needs dwell upon the high places of the earth, you shall find the mountain summits cold and barren: the Lord dwells with the lowly, but He knows the proud afar off.

Charles Spurgeon[2]

6

The Fire of Humility

During a visit to Nigeria in 2003, I was asked to speak at a conference in downtown Lagos. The meeting was to take place at the Muson Centre, a fancy civic auditorium, and I was told that several prominent church leaders would be in the audience. Of course it would require me to wear a suit, since all Nigerian Christians wear their Sunday best on such occasions.

Around 4 p.m. my friends picked me up and we began the drive from Lekki, a nearby suburb. Unfortunately, "nearby" in Lagos can mean more than an hour in the car—most of which is sitting in standstill traffic in 95-degree heat. While it is a city of nine million, Lagos had only a few dozen working traffic lights at that time. Intersections are always snarled. Getting anywhere often requires miraculous intervention.

Sure enough, we hit a nightmarish jam and we found ourselves stranded in a cloud of dust and exhaust fumes. My friends began to call people at the convention hall to discuss alternate routes. Then they began to discuss alternate modes of transportation. (Someone even suggested using a boat to cross the lake near the intersection where we were trapped!)

As I listened to the phone conversations, I heard someone mention "Okada." I figured this must be the driver who was coming to rescue us. I was looking forward to greeting Mr. Okada. Then my friend Andy explained that *okada* was not a person but a form of transportation. It is, in fact, the poor man's taxi, a crude motorcycle that whisks only the bravest and most desperate travelers to their destinations.

Before I had a chance to weigh my options, the *okada* arrived. The driver was not wearing a helmet, and he did not offer me one. He revved his motor and smiled wickedly, as if to say, "Come and join me on your journey to certain death."

I breathed a prayer and then straddled the vinyl seat, holding onto my driver for dear life. Within seconds we were weaving between cars at a fast clip, stirring up red dust and attracting curious glances from the locals. The sight of a white guy in a black suit barreling through town on the back of a motorcycle taxi must have looked like a scene from a Nigerian comedy film.

I opened my eyes a few times, only to see that we were headed into a two-foot-wide space between two buses that were inching closer to each other by the second. I squeezed my driver tighter, groaned and shut my eyes again. The driver again laughed and sped onward.

I began to think of my mother. Every time I go to Africa she worries that I will die. "I am not telling my mother about this," I said aloud. Nobody heard me. The scratchy roar of the cycle's engine seemed to drown out all other noises in Lagos.

We weaved through more traffic, jumped on and off sidewalks, squeezed through more intersections and finally pulled in front of the Muson Centre—where many of the bishops of Lagos were waiting for me, "the man of God," to arrive with the usual "entourage."

114

These dignified Africans got the shock of their lives. I drove up on the back of an *okada*, my suit and shoes covered with dust. It could have been an embarrassing scene, but as soon as I stepped off the cycle and said good-bye to my driver (and thanked him for sparing my life) I recognized this was a prophetic moment.

When I took the podium that evening, I told my Nigerian hosts that my unorthodox arrival was actually full of relevant meaning. I apologized to them for the way some American ministers have demanded limousines, red carpets and celebrity treatment. And I exhorted them to renounce the arrogance, pride and entitlement that characterize so much of Western Christianity.

I reminded the Nigerians that when Jesus came into the world, He made His first appearance in a lowly manger—in a place that smelled of sheep and cows. Just days before His crucifixion, He entered Jerusalem on a humble donkey that He had to borrow from residents of a poor village (Matthew 21:1–4). He did not demand fancy horses, regal guards or trumpet blasts. He did not expect royal treatment. He laid aside His kingly glory and took on the form of a bondservant.

The whole experience in Nigeria taught me an important lesson. If Jesus had visited Lagos, He probably would have used an *okada*. It's a lesson we sophisticated Christians in the 21st century should ponder.

The Deadly Virus of Celebrity Christianity

Since my experience in Nigeria, I've learned that a deadly new strain of pride is spreading through large segments of the charismatic movement. One friend of mine in Texas recently inquired to see if a prominent preacher could speak at her conference. The minister's assistant faxed back a list of requirements that had to be met in order to book a speaking engagement. The demands included:

- a five-figure honorarium
- a $10,000 gasoline deposit for the private plane
- a hairstylist for the speaker
- a suite in a five-star hotel
- a luxury car from the airport to the hotel (the make and model were specified)
- room-temperature Perrier water

I was relieved to know that this celebrity preacher's requirements in 2007 did not include a set of armed bodyguards—because I would have been tempted to jump uninvited into their Rolls-Royce and say a few words to him.

The virus actually gets worse, if you can believe it. At a charismatic conference in an East Coast city in 2009, a pastor stood in front of a large crowd and smugly announced that the guest speaker was "more than an apostle." Then the host asked everyone to bow down to the person, claiming that this posture was necessary to release God's power.

"This is the only way you can receive this kind of anointing!" the host declared, bowing in front of the speaker. Immediately, about 80 percent of the audience fell prostrate on the floor. The few who were uncomfortable with these weird spiritual-control proceedings either stood in silent protest or walked out.

In this case, it wasn't enough to feed a celebrity preacher's ego by treating him like a rock star. The people were also required to worship him.

In some places you have to pay big bucks to speak with a celebrity preacher. In a city in the South, a well-known preacher was known to ask for money in order to secure a five- or ten-minute counseling session. The minister uses Proverbs 18:16, "A man's gift makes room for him and brings him before great men," to support this bizarre practice. Some people are known to give more than $1,000 for a short meeting.

People on fixed incomes need not apply for this kind of elite ministry. People, that is, like lepers, blind beggars, Samaritan women and any of the other social outcasts who were welcomed and healed by Jesus without payment.

What has become of the American church? What is this sickness spreading in the Body of Christ? I don't know whom to blame more for it: the narcissistic minister who craves the attention, or the spiritually naïve crowds who place these arrogant people on their shaky pedestals. All I know is that God is grieved by this shameful carnality.

How far we have fallen from authentic New Testament faith. Paul, who carried the anointing of an apostle but often described himself as a bondslave, told the Thessalonians, "Having so fond an affection for you, we were well-pleased to impart to you not only the gospel of God but also our own lives" (1 Thessalonians 2:8).

New Testament Christianity is humble, selfless and authentic. And messengers of Gospel truth don't preach for selfish gain or to meet an emotional need for attention. May God help us root out the false apostles and false teachers who are making the American church sick with man-centered, money-focused heresies.

A Return to Relational Christianity

A friend in Alabama recently told me about a preacher who came to his city in unusual style. The man arrived at a church in a limousine and was whisked into a private waiting room behind the stage area. The evangelist gave specific instructions to leave his limousine's engine running (I guess he wasn't concerned about rising gas prices) so that the temperature inside his car would remain constant.

This evangelist preached to the waiting crowd, took up his own offering and retired to the waiting room for some refreshments. Then he left the church with his entourage without even speaking to the host pastor.

This man's "faith" message—he is touted as a faith preacher—may have been inspiring, but his love was as cold as the air inside his oversized vehicle. His behavior that night represents why so many ministries today are in crisis. We've created a monster—a version of Christianity that is slick, marketable and event-driven but lacking in any authentic impact. It is as one-dimensional as a flat-screen TV— and a total turnoff to people who are starving for genuine relationships.

This preacher's detached style is the exact opposite of the apostle Paul's. His deep relational bond with his mentees is reflected in all his epistles. He almost slobbers as he describes his affection for his ministry team in the sixteenth chapter of Romans. When he says good-bye to his colleagues in Ephesus they weep and kiss each other. He tells the Philippians: "I have you in my heart" (1:7).

And he conveys uninhibited affection when he greets the Thessalonians. Note how *The Message* translates his words: "Even though we had some standing as Christ's apostles, we never threw our weight around or tried to come across as important, with you or anyone else. We weren't aloof with you. We took you just as you were. We were never patronizing, never condescending, but we cared for you the way a mother cares for her children. We loved you dearly. Not content to just pass on the Message, we wanted to give you our hearts. And we *did*" (1 Thessalonians 2:6–8).

Paul's ministry style is best visible in his relationship with his spiritual son Timothy, who often traveled with him. More than one-fourth of the 27 books in the New Testament are either written by Paul to Timothy or by Paul and Timothy to various churches (2 Corinthians, Philippians, Colossians, 1 and 2 Thessalonians, and Philemon). This clearly signals that genuine Christianity is not about the things attendant to a sole figure and his gifts or anointing. It has everything to do with close teamwork.

But how can we reclaim this style of relational Christianity? How can we resist the carnal egotism that has overtaken so much of our movement? We would be wise to take these steps:

First, we must become accessible. Jesus modeled accessibility against a backdrop of an austere religious culture. The rabbis in Jesus' day were obsessed with their robes, titles and public pontifications while they stayed away from the common people. Meanwhile, Jesus held children in His arms, ate with reviled tax collectors and showed affection to His disciples.

Over the past thirty years many of our churches have developed a sterile religious culture that keeps leaders elevated and separated from their congregations. Thankfully, the younger generation is rejecting this because they can see the emperor has no clothes. Churches that want to grow in this current season—and that want to reach the younger generation—will have to ditch these old paradigms, along with the teachings that created them.

Second, we must open up our lives. I regularly meet ministry leaders who tell me they have no friends. Some feel threatened by the idea of a group of superiors who might dominate or control them. Others fear that if they admit struggles or weaknesses, they will lose their jobs. Others have never had a spiritual father or significant mentor.

They are relationally empty. They have nothing to impart but three-point sermons and motivational principles. They may shout praises on Sunday morning but they struggle with loneliness on Sunday night.

I have often challenged groups of Christian men about their need for friendship. I tell them that every man needs three types of relationships in his life: a "Paul," a "Barnabas" and a "Timothy." Pauls are mentors and spiritual fathers. Barnabases are peers who are on our level and relate to us as close friends. Timothys are younger spiritual sons whom we can disciple and encourage.

Sadly, when I bring up this subject, often the men admit they have none of these relationships in their lives.

This dam must break. Hearts must open, honest confession must flow and godly friendships must be forged if we hope to offer healing to our fractured, love-starved generation. Church should be the ultimate place where people can find connection—not just with God but also with each other.

Third, we must develop effective discipleship models. In all the countries I have visited I've never seen a healthy, growing church that didn't have an organic small-group system. Real disciples are not made on an assembly line; they are fashioned with loving care in intimate, relational settings. And this kind of ministry requires humility because the leader must take a backseat and allow his or her congregation to do most of the work of ministry. The senior pastor cannot be the star of the show.

One of the main reasons I am serving God today is that a youth leader named Barry St. Clair took me under his wing when I was fourteen and nurtured me in a small group Bible study for more than three years. Barry, at age thirty, was already a successful author and speaker and a busy husband and father, but he took the time to invest in a Southern Baptist teenager by including me on ministry trips and praying with me about personal problems.

Barry became my most trusted counselor after I went into ministry. He stood with me at my wedding. He prayed over me at my ordination. He still writes me encouraging notes—35 years after he taught me to have a quiet time with God.

Today we need to get back to these very kinds of basics. After the inaccessible preachers have driven off in their limousines, we are still called to make disciples. And we can't fulfill that mandate until we stop the ego show and embrace a humble ministry style that puts relationships first.

Pride as Spiritual Abuse

What all of us charismatics and Pentecostals must learn is that egotism is a form of spiritual abuse and prostitution—an illegal means to self-gratification at the expense of others. God-fearing church leaders should do whatever necessary to avoid this trap.

The apostle Paul instructed Timothy not to select unproven, spiritually immature men to oversee the church. Such novices, he warned, may "become conceited and fall into the condemnation incurred by the devil" (1 Timothy 3:6). Conceit is a fatal attraction lurking in the shadows of the Church. If unseasoned leaders are allowed to flirt with it, they bring not only condemnation on themselves but havoc on their congregations.

It may seem alarming that in his letter to Timothy, Paul compared egotistical ministers to Satan himself. But Satan's ultimate sin, after all, was pride. Not satisfied to share an exalted place in heaven as an anointed angelic being, he wanted to build his own kingdom. Weary of worshiping God, he wanted worship for himself.

This is also the motive of the egotistical minister or evangelist, whether or not he is aware of it. And the result is clear in the "fruit" that results from his "ministry." People who show up at services or meetings are used to help build attendance figures. Parishioners or followers with money are used to help fill the collection plate and pay for his TV ministry, expensive foreign car or Italian designer suit. People who think he is God's special messenger will do anything to help him build his own kingdom—without even knowing they're doing it.

When we tolerate this kind of ego trip, it leads to more serious forms of abuse, such as sexual sin and financial mismanagement. Leaders accustomed to using people to satisfy their own egos develop a tolerance for using people in many ways, without pausing to consider their calling to serve them.

121

This is what happened in part to fallen televangelist Jim Bakker and his ministry. The entire Praise The Lord (PTL) empire had been built around the personalities of Jim and his wife, Tammy Faye, and donors were eager to give to support the notion that the ministry was making a dramatic difference. But the hype and flashy promotions got so bad that Christian journalist Jamie Buckingham was moved to describe the Bakkers' TV program as "an hour-long real estate commercial" and "a charismatic version of Romper Room."[3]

PTL donors eventually learned that they were being drained of their funds to satisfy Jim Bakker's cravings for acceptance. PTL was a house of cards built on dishonest claims, and it came crashing down in 1987. By the time Hurricane Hugo swept through Charlotte, North Carolina, in 1989, causing damage to Bakker's then-vacant Heritage USA complex, thousands of Christians had come to terms with the fact that they had been used.

Despite Bakker's sexual encounter with former church secretary Jessica Hahn, the PTL fiasco was far more than a sex scandal. Whatever sexual misconduct had occurred inside or outside PTL was only a manifestation of the root problem: an inflated ego and a propensity to abuse. The PTL fiasco, like many scandals in the Church since, was caused by egotism.

I see a charismatic church today that is tired of kingdom-building and personality-driven ministry. We are less prone now to being dragged around to fulfill someone's so-called vision. We are more leery of wasting God's money on monuments to the flesh, and weary of being manipulated into being part of someone's personal agenda. Some Christians who have been abused in one way or another by egotistical Church leaders have been so hurt—and this is the saddest part of the story—they will have nothing more to do with the established Church. Rather than repeatedly apply forgiveness, many have become bitter and refuse to trust Christians altogether.

The only solution is for Christian leaders to make a renewed commitment to humility. Those of us in any leadership role in the Church must stop viewing the people of God as a means to gratify ourselves. We must repent of fleecing the flock and ask God to forgive us for pursuing our own agendas rather than His.

Pride is actually more than abuse; it is insanity. Egotism unchecked actually becomes a form of mental illness—a point bracingly illustrated in the story of King Nebuchadnezzar. The prophet tells us that Nebuchadnezzar lost control of himself after he allowed pride to overtake him. He said:

> [King Nebuchadnezzar] said, "Is not this the great Babylon I have built as the royal residence, by my mighty power and for the glory of my majesty?"
>
> The words were still on his lips when a voice came from heaven, "This is what is decreed for you, King Nebuchadnezzar: Your royal authority has been taken from you. You will be driven away from people and will live with the wild animals, you will eat grass like cattle. Seven times will pass by for you until you acknowledge that the Most High is sovereign over the kingdoms of men and gives them to anyone he wishes."
>
> Daniel 4:30–32, NIV

Immediately what had been said about Nebuchadnezzar was fulfilled. The king was driven away from people and was reduced to eating grass like cattle. Scripture's description is that Nebuchadnezzar's body was drenched with the dew of heaven until his hair grew like the feathers of an eagle and his nails like the claws of a bird. In short, he lived like a madman.

Pride makes human beings crazy. God humbled Nebuchadnezzar by making him lose his mind, and the mighty king learned the hard way that he was the creature after all and not the Creator.

Over the years I have watched many charismatic and Pentecostal leaders strut across platforms with a haughtiness similar to Nebuchadnezzar's. They have exulted in their anointing, announced their power over demonic strongholds, threatened to call down God's judgment at their own discretion and used their ostensible spiritual power to manipulate—even intimidate—their audiences. I cringe when I see this, because I know these men and women are setting up their audiences for abuse and setting themselves up for a fall.

The Mark of the Beast

A monster called Leviathan is described in the book of Job as a beast so fierce that his crashing caused even the mightiest to fear. This was no ordinary animal, according to the description: "Nothing on earth is his equal—a creature without fear. He looks down on all that are haughty; he is king over all that are proud" (Job 41:33–34, NIV).

The creature was apparently one of the fiercest and most dreaded animals ever known. He seemed invincible. His reptilian armor was impenetrable. When he finally surfaced to breathe, his huge frame, usually hidden under the ocean depths, was horrible to behold. This monster was a master of terror:

> Who can strip off his outer coat?
>> Who would approach him with a bridle?
> Who dares open the doors of his mouth,
>> ringed about with his fearsome teeth? . . .
> Strength resides in his neck;
>> dismay goes before him. . . .
> The sword that reaches him has no effect,
>> nor does the spear or the dart or the javelin.
> Iron he treats like straw
>> and bronze like rotten wood. . . .

A club seems to him but a piece of straw;
he laughs at the rattling of the lance.

Job 41:13–14, 22, 26–27, 29, NIV

Leviathan no longer lives on the earth.[4] Changes in the earth's climate after the flood of Noah's day probably drove the creature to extinction. But the spirit of Leviathan lives on. This invincible animal who terrorized humanity but was finally wiped out by God represents the spirit of pride, the force that inflates human egos to lofty proportions and tempts us to live as if we were self-sufficient.

There is no question that in American society the spirit of Leviathan flourishes. We have become a nation of success addicts and overachievers. Winning is everything. The business world emphasizes the biggest, the best, the hottest and the fastest, enticing America to an endless pursuit of first place. The healthy competition that stimulates a free economy has given way to an incessant striving to achieve, regardless of moral principles or the cost to others.

Sadly, this "pride of life" is equally evident in many of our churches. We are gripped by a spirit of self-promotion. Church growth has become less a matter of winning individual souls to Christ than an impersonal numbers game. We have become proud, self-sufficient and insensitive to people's needs.

This spirit of pride is manifested in three ways:

1. A lack of servanthood. Jesus told His disciples they should call no one either "father" or "teacher" (Matthew 23:9–10). He also explained to them that the Christian idea of leadership is contrary to the pagan concept. "Whoever wants to become great among you," He told them, "must be your servant, and whoever wants to be first must be your slave—just as the Son of Man did not come to be served, but to serve, and to give his life as a ransom for many" (Matthew 20:26–28, NIV).

The Christian concept of leadership conflicts with the accepted ideas of Western culture. Servanthood is not the American way. We like the concept of the rugged individual who pulls himself up by his bootstraps. We make gods of our heroes. Like the ancient Greeks, from whom we borrowed so much of our current thought, we still worship the image of the god-man. Adonis, Apollo and Aphrodite are still competing in our stadiums, performing in Hollywood or topping the Fortune 500 listing.

Many passages in the New Testament seem to have been written to address the superstar syndrome. Paul hammered continually on the theme that the Kingdom of God is composed of many interdependent members. We all have different functions and we all need each other. The teenager who picks up the trash after the worship service is as important as the most talented speaker.

But because the pagan idea of leadership pervades our churches, many of us are in constant pursuit of celebrity status in the Kingdom of God. Rather than seek the favor of God, we seek the recognition of others. We prefer to rule rather than to serve. We are moved not because we want to meet the needs of others, but because we want to be admired by them. We are settling for success in the eyes of men rather than a heavenly reward.

2. An overemphasis on personal greatness. The American church has heard plenty of teaching in recent years about personal destiny, reminding us that God has a calling on every person in His Kingdom. Most of this has been beneficial; but we must take care that our teaching about destiny does not degenerate into a lust for greatness. We must constantly place our desires for recognition (or significance or power or fame) on the altar. Even Christian ministry can become an idol in our lives and keep us from being used by the Holy Spirit.

Paul exhorted us to have the attitude that was in Jesus Christ: "Do nothing out of selfish ambition or vain conceit, but in humility consider others better than yourselves. Each of you should look not only to your own interests, but also to the interests of others" (Philippians 2:3–4, NIV).

Jesus was tempted, before He began His ministry, to accomplish His mission Satan's way. He could have proclaimed Himself the ruler of all the kingdoms of the world, and Satan would have granted Him more honor and fame than any earthly king has ever known. But Jesus rejected the devil's method for greatness. The path He chose to walk was one of humility, self-denial, even obscurity. He would die virtually unknown.

Jesus told His followers they must follow the same path. To seek our *own* life, He said—to pursue advancement, promotion or fame in the eyes of others—is to forfeit fruitfulness in His Kingdom. A seed, before it can produce anything, must die in the ground.

All of us in the charismatic renewal need a swift return to these simple truths of self-denial. We need to learn humility. Rather than emphasize the need to fulfill our own destinies, those of us in any form of ministry need to view our primary calling as that of equipping others to achieve their full potential.

3. Competition within churches and among Christian leaders. Paul also said that Jesus came to earth in the form of a bondservant, and that He "did not regard equality with God a thing to be grasped" (Philippians 2:6). Grasping for power and position among leaders, by contrast, has become commonplace.

Walls of isolation and division have been fortified between and even within denominations as leaders compete for the title of biggest and best. Rather than link arms to achieve a common goal, we have pursued the largest congregations, the best buildings, the biggest mailing lists, the most television time. In our zeal to "kick in the gates of hell" and "stay on the cutting edge," we have lost sight of the humble nature of our Leader.

Our Western philosophy, so steeped in competitive tradition, has done plenty to squelch true fellowship and love in our churches. Leaders find it hard to express genuine affection for one another. Pastors stand aloof from their congregations and from each other because this subtle competitive spirit prevents a sincere expression of brotherhood. And the Holy Spirit is prevented from moving among us in this restrictive atmosphere.

Happily, there is increasing cooperation among certain Christian ministries and churches that we did not see even ten years ago. Pentecostals who have typically been isolationist are working with other evangelicals. Parachurch ministries such as Youth With A Mission and Campus Crusade for Christ are cooperating with denominations. Partnering is now more common in the missions community.

When Jesus spent His last evening with His disciples, He laid aside His garments, dressed like a servant with a single towel around His waist and washed the feet of His friends. Then He gave them this charge: "Now that I, your Lord and Teacher, have washed your feet, you also should wash one another's feet. I have set you an example that you should do as I have done for you" (John 13:14–15, NIV). Jesus did not call the disciples and incite them to compete for first place. Rather, He demonstrated to them that the battle would be won only through mutual love, covenant, cooperation and transparent relationships.

If charismatics and Pentecostals set servanthood, humility and mutual cooperation as our goals, we will see fruitfulness on a scale we could hardly now imagine.

Questions for Discussion

1. In what ways do you believe Jesus modeled true humility?
2. In what ways do people feed the deadly virus of celebrity Christianity? How can we stop it?

3. In what ways do you experience "relational Christianity"? Do you have a "Paul," a "Barnabas" and a "Timothy" in your life?
4. Why is it so important for us to allow the Holy Spirit to deal with our pride?
5. How does Jesus' act of washing His disciples' feet speak to us today about our ministry values?

Preach the word; be ready in season and out of season; reprove, rebuke, exhort, with great patience and instruction. For the time will come when they will not endure sound doctrine; but wanting to have their ears tickled, they will accumulate for themselves teachers in accordance to their own desires, and will turn away their ears from the truth and will turn aside to myths.

2 Timothy 4:2–4

Rest assured that the most fervid revivalism will wear itself out in mere smoke, if it be not maintained by the fuel of teaching. . . . Sound teaching is the best protection for the heresies which ravage right and left among us.

Charles Spurgeon[1]

There is so little discernment left in the church among so many pastors and even church leaders. They don't even know when the Holy Ghost is being misrepresented or blasphemed. There are thousands of Christians who go to crusades and they see things that they think are the Holy Ghost and they don't even know what they are sitting under. They are clapping and praising God while a man stands up there blaspheming and misrepresenting the Holy Ghost and they don't even know it. Folks, what we are seeing today in what is called so many revivals and things that are happening attributed to the Holy Ghost cannot be found in the Scripture. Anything that cannot be found in this Book has to be rejected outright. Totally rejected!

Revivalist David Wilkerson[2]

7

The Fire of Truth

When I began making regular ministry trips to Nigeria a few years ago, I learned that a peculiar Nigerian minister named T. B. Joshua was causing quite a stir in that country. Often referred to as "the Man of God" or "the Man in the Synagogue" by his followers, this African preacher founded a massive religious compound in Lagos called The Synagogue Church of All Nations. He began attracting big crowds because of his supposed healing powers.

I was initially excited to hear about a new healing ministry on the international scene, but when I talked to pastors in Lagos I learned that no mainstream Christian church or denomination in Nigeria embraced Joshua as authentic. In fact, Pentecostal and charismatic leaders had denounced him publicly because of his occult background and because he mixed Christian terminology with pagan healing methods.

I finally sat down with Joshua in 2003 to confront him about his story (including his claim that his mother carried him in the womb for fifteen months because he was "special"). After being in his offices, talking with his zombielike followers, interviewing ex-members of his cult and watching videos of his bizarre methods (that include a form of "magic writing"), my own gut feelings confirmed what I had already been told by countless pastors in Lagos, Port Harcourt, Abuja and other cities: This man was not operating by the Holy Spirit's power.

More confirmation came when I met a young Nigerian man named Bayo who had served as T. B. Joshua's valet for several months. Bayo confirmed how Joshua mixed Christian teaching with African spiritism—and he told me horror stories of how Joshua's zealous followers had tried to kill Bayo when he escaped from the Synagogue to become a Christian.

What was even more shocking was seeing planeloads of Christians from South Africa, Europe and North America arriving in Nigeria to attend T. B. Joshua's meetings. The excited pilgrims came to receive a touch from God. They wanted a spiritual impartation. Some left claiming they had been healed.

It was through this experience that I realized how desperately devoid of discernment the American church has become. Western Christians who watched T. B. Joshua perform miracles assumed his power was from God; after all, in the United States we are not used to seeing these demonstrations of the supernatural. In Africa, of course, Christians know that the devil has power, too—and that they must differentiate between God's miracles and Satan's lying wonders. It is a lesson we must learn.

When the charismatic movement was at its zenith thirty years ago, Christians rediscovered the gifts of the Holy Spirit listed in the apostle Paul's letter to the Corinthians. We embraced healing, prophecy, speaking in tongues and miracles—gifts that had been ignored by the mainline church for centuries.

We also learned that discernment is one of these nine supernatural gifts (1 Corinthians 12:8–10). We were taught that because the devil has the ability to counterfeit, and because Satan's activity includes "all power and signs and false wonders" (2 Thessalonians 2:9), God's people must be equipped with supernatural power to tell the difference between the true and the false.

God gave us spiritual gifts in a package, and discernment is part of the set. It is not optional. Yet today it seems we've set discernment aside—perhaps because we're suspicious of any gift that requires us to exercise clear judgment and sort right from wrong.

We live in a confusing season marked by spiritual compromise, moral relativism and deceptive imitations. Television host Oprah Winfrey tells the world that Jesus is not the only way to God. She suggests that spirituality is up for grabs and that you can define it however you want. The broad way to destruction is celebrated while the narrow way to salvation is criticized. Anyone who believes in the narrow is branded narrow-minded.

And in some charismatic churches, hunger for the supernatural is encouraged while leaders seem reluctant to put biblical boundaries around it for fear of seeming intolerant. We stopped teaching discernment because it forces us to draw lines. We desperately need to return to what the Bible teaches us about this important subject.

We must remember that we are *commanded* to discern. The apostle John instructed us to "test the spirits to see whether they are from God, because many false prophets have gone out into the world" (1 John 4:1). We don't like to test because it seems harsh. We don't like confrontation. We want to be nice to everybody. But it is the Lord who tells us to test the spirits. Will we please people or fear God?

Discernment is a sign of spiritual maturity. The author of Hebrews told his readers that they were immature babies who couldn't handle eating spiritual meat. "Solid food is for the mature, who because of practice have their senses trained *to discern good and evil*" (Hebrews 5:14, emphasis added). The implication here is that those who don't learn to discern are spiritually stunted.

Is it possible we have been so focused on satisfying our own material or emotional needs that we have gotten stuck in perpetual infancy? The Bible offers a remedy: Grow up! We will never come to full adulthood in a spiritual sense if we don't develop discernment.

We must understand that discernment is damaged when leaders compromise. The prophet Ezekiel denounced the priests and governors of Israel because they didn't teach the people to discern. "They have made no distinction between the holy and the profane, and they have not taught the difference between the unclean and the clean" (Ezekiel 22:26). Discernment, according to this passage, is shaped by the choices leaders make.

When shepherds don't build fences, sheep wander into wolves' territory. That's why God holds leaders to a stricter standard. In some cases today, leaders have brought their flocks to feed near toxic streams. The Gospel has been polluted by false prophecies and poisonous doctrines and, in some tragic cases, by the immorality and greed imparted from the pulpit.

Do you want the gift of discernment? Be warned: It will probably not make you popular. But I pray we will be willing to risk our popularity in order to become mature disciples of Jesus—and to guard the American church from deception.

A Tragedy in Lakeland

Canadian evangelist Todd Bentley had heralded the much-touted Lakeland Revival as the greatest Pentecostal outpouring since Azusa Street. From his stage in a gigantic tent in Florida, Bentley preached to thousands, bringing many of them to the stage for prayer. Many claimed to be healed of deafness, blindness, heart problems, depression and dozens of other conditions in the Lakeland services, which ran for more than one hundred consecutive nights. Bentley announced confidently that dozens of people had been raised from the dead during the revival.

From the first week of the Lakeland meetings, many discerning Christians raised questions about Bentley's beliefs and practices. They felt uneasy when he said he talked to an angel in his hotel room. They sensed something was amiss when he wore a T-shirt with a skeleton on it. They wondered why a man of God would cover himself with tattoos. They were horrified when they heard him describe how he tackled a man and knocked out his tooth during prayer.

Bentley's popularity grew because the Lakeland meetings were aired live every night on television. But concerns grew as people researched some of his writings. They learned that he had claimed to make frequent trips to the third heaven, where he supposedly talked to the apostle Paul. Bentley also wrote extensively about angels, including a female angel named Emma whom he said wore a flowing, white gown and resembled evangelist Kathryn Kuhlman.

I went to one of the meetings in Lakeland with an open mind. I saw many sincerely passionate Christians who love God. I know they came to those meetings in faith for healing and spiritual renewal—and many of them left feeling refreshed. Any time you gather that many Christians in one place, you will sense God's presence.

But I could not shake the feeling that something wasn't right. I didn't want to judge Bentley just because he had tattoos. I wanted to cheer Bentley on simply because I knew he appealed to a younger crowd—and I want to reach them. But still, something seemed off-base.

I could tell that my own gift of discernment was sending a signal. There was something impure in the atmosphere. When I read Bentley's writings, heard him speak and watched videos of him praying, I knew the Holy Spirit was sending me a warning. What convinced me was when I saw a video clip of Bentley teaching about how to pray for the sick. He told the crowd in Lakeland how God had instructed him while in Canada to kick a woman with his biker boot. Bentley told the audience. "And God said, kick that woman in the face!"[3]

The people roared with laughter. I was grieved. How could anyone take this man seriously when his style of ministry was actually encouraging violence?

But the people went along with Bentley for months. For those who jumped on the Lakeland bandwagon, discernment was discouraged. They were expected to swallow and follow. The message was clear: "This is God. Don't question." I blame this lack of discernment, partly, on raw zeal for God. We're spiritually hungry, which can be a good thing. But sometimes, hungry people will eat anything.

Things got very strange when television viewers were told by network hosts in a prebroadcast show that any criticism of Todd Bentley and the Lakeland Revival was "demonic." In fact, network hosts also warned listeners that if they listened to criticism of Bentley they could lose their healings.

This was cultic manipulation at its worst. The Bible tells us that the Bereans were noble believers because they studied the Scriptures daily "to see whether these things were so" (Acts 17:11). Yet in the case of Lakeland, honest biblical inquiry was viewed as a sign of weakness. People were expected to jump first and then open their eyes.

The Lakeland Revival took a bizarre twist in its third month when a group of respected charismatic leaders decided to publicly commission Bentley as an evangelist and provide him with "apostolic covering." I was asked to be a part of this ceremony, but I refused on the grounds that I had too many questions about Bentley's theology, integrity and methods. But a large group of leaders gathered around Bentley on a July evening and—on live television—proclaimed that he was a great revival leader.

They praised him. They prophesied that he would influence nations. One woman even prophesied that no man since Moses had caught God's attention as much as Bentley. The whole evening looked more like the coronation of a king than the commissioning of a minister.

I have never been more disappointed in leaders I respected than I was that night. I couldn't believe they were giving Bentley this kind of blanket endorsement when there were so many question marks surrounding him. Why did these leaders do this? I can only assume it was a lack of godly discernment. (To be fair, one of the leaders still contends that God directed him to commission Bentley, and maintained that it was the commissioning that actually exposed Bentley's sin a few days later.)

Bentley certainly needed apostolic covering. No one in ministry today should be out on their own, living in isolation without checks, balances and wise counsel. It was commendable that these leaders reached out to Bentley and that Bentley acknowledged his need for spiritual fathers by agreeing to submit to the process. I maintain it would have been better to take Bentley into a back room and discuss with him all those questions.

The Bible tells us that ordination of a minister is a sober responsibility. Paul wrote: "Do not lay hands upon anyone too hastily and thereby share responsibility for the sins of others" (1 Timothy 5:22). We might be tempted to rush the process, but the apostle warned against fast-tracking ordination. And he said that those who commission a minister who is not ready for the job will bear some of the blame for his failures.

In the end, those who had questions about Bentley understood why. After four months of nonstop services, Bentley abruptly vanished. Then he resurfaced, apologizing to his fans and explaining that he was having marriage problems. He admitted that he was burned out from all the meetings. Then, within months, it was revealed that he had left his wife and married a young woman who had worked with his ministry as an intern.

Some people were disgusted. Many felt betrayed. And a lot of the young people who thought Bentley's stage antics were real felt disillusioned. Because of Bentley's actions and the poor judgment of well-known charismatic leaders, the faith of many will end up in shipwreck. Some may give up on church and join the growing ranks of Christians bitter and disenfranchised over just such scandals. This could have been avoided if leaders had been more vocal about their objections and urged people to evaluate spiritual experiences through the filter of God's Word.

A prominent evangelist called me a week after Bentley's news became public. He said soberly: "I'm now convinced that a large segment of the charismatic church will follow the Antichrist when he shows up because they have no discernment."

Ouch. Hopefully we'll have learned our lesson the next time an imposter shows up and apply the necessary caution.

Please hear me. Just because we believe in the power of the Holy Spirit does not mean we check our brains at the church door. We are commanded to test the spirits. Jesus wants us to love Him with our hearts *and* our minds. In fact, it is mandatory to use our God-given intellect to study doctrine and weigh evidence.

It is tragic that some of us would rather watch a noisy demonstration of miracles, signs and wonders than have a quiet Bible study. Yet we are faced today with the sad reality that our untempered zeal is a sign of immaturity. Our adolescent craving for the wild and crazy makes us do stupid things. It's way past time for us to grow up.

False Angels, Spiritual Flakes and Charismatic Chaos

Noncharismatics who are sympathetic to the charismatic renewal believe that one of the primary purposes of the Pentecostal outpouring at the beginning of the twentieth century was to bring about in the Church a restoration of the gifts of the Holy Spirit. Although many evangelical denominations still subscribe to the belief that the spiritual gifts listed in 1 Corinthians 12 are no longer in operation,[4] a growing percentage of believers today have come to accept prophecy, healing, speaking in tongues and other *charismata* as valid expressions of the Spirit's work.

Indeed, this belief in the gifts of the Spirit is central to understanding the dynamic growth of the charismatic movement and its popular appeal. The typical charismatic or Pentecostal believer trusts in a God who is actively at work in the world today. Charismatic Christians maintain that Jesus Christ still speaks, still heals the sick, still delivers the oppressed from demonic torment. The Christ who walked the streets of Galilee two thousand years ago "is the same yesterday and today and forever" (Hebrews 13:8), and He expresses His life through His indwelling Spirit in the Church. Supernatural healings, divine guidance and miraculous answers to prayer are viewed as clear evidence of Christ's modern-day ministry on earth.

Yet at the same time that the gifts of the Spirit have been reclaimed by Christians worldwide, they also have been misused and abused, either intentionally by charlatans or unintentionally by misguided believers. The giftings of God, intended to strengthen the faith of individual Christians and equip the Church for the task of world evangelization, have been prostituted for personal gain and cheapened in the eyes of the Church and the world. In some cases, the abuse of spiritual gifts has so repulsed believers that it has triggered a backlash against the very renewal of the Church.

The essence of the charismatic experience requires openness to God's supernatural workings. Yet such openness poses potential problems and requires believers to exercise careful discernment. While the apostle Paul exhorted his followers to exercise spiritual gifts (he himself claimed to have seen visions and experienced other supernatural phenomena), he also cautioned the early Church to test the validity of prophecies, visions and angelic visitations (1 Corinthians 12:1–3; 14:6–40; Galatians 1:6–9).

We know from Paul's admonitions to the Corinthians, for example, that the believers there were misusing the gift of tongues, promoting heretical doctrines in their "prophecies" and constantly interrupting church meetings to convey unorthodox "revelations."

Paul warned the Colossians that they were in danger of being defrauded by people claiming to have exclusive access to divine revelation or special spiritual power. He told them, "Do not let anyone who delights in false humility and the worship of angels disqualify you for the prize. Such a person goes into great detail about what he has seen, and his unspiritual mind puffs him up with idle notions" (Colossians 2:18, NIV). The church in Colosse apparently had a problem with self-proclaimed mystics who believed they were called by God to impose their perverse views on the congregation. Churches are always debilitated, sometimes irreparably, when this kind of misguided mysticism continues unchecked.

The confusion that characterized the churches at Corinth and Colosse resembles the current state of affairs in the indigenous underground house churches in the People's Republic of China. Although the Church in that country is growing explosively, the lack of Bibles and trained leaders has produced a movement fraught with heresy, doctrinal division and bizarre practices. One fast-growing house church movement in China teaches that only those believers who have heard the voice of God audibly can be assured of salvation. Another group teaches that the Holy Spirit can be invoked when believers remove their clothes and dance together.[5]

These may seem like outlandish examples, but Pentecostals in the United States have promoted equally ridiculous doctrines by way of visions, dreams and "words from the Lord." Entire denominations have split over foolish directives given by hyperspiritual mystics who claim an inside connection to the Holy Spirit.

One of the most dangerous trends that has surfaced in charismatic churches in recent days relates to the ministry of angels. At a growing Brazilian church in Boston, a pastor told his congregation he was having regular conversations with an angel. Weeks later he set a chair on the stage for the heavenly visitor, whom he said was attending Sunday services even though no one could see him.

The pastor eventually wrote a book containing messages he had supposedly received from the angel. The man's teachings became so bizarre that he was eventually removed from his denomination for promoting heresy.

That scenario may seem extreme, but it is one example of widespread emphasis on angels and angelic encounters in the charismatic movement today. In the case of the Brazilian church, the pastor went off the theological deep end and his church became a cult. It remains to be seen what will happen in other sectors of the charismatic movement as leaders promote teachings about angels that range from the mildly weird to downright wacky.

For example, a young evangelist who was preaching in Canada in 2008 held up a jar with a feather in it and told the congregation it belonged to an angel who visits him. He said the angel was coming to the service to release riches and healing to those who wanted prayer.

It is popular in some circles to speak of angels that bring healing, wealth or special anointings. Some have described angels as tall as skyscrapers while others say they have seen tiny angels the size of insects. One prophet spoke of angels who are sleeping inside the walls of churches. Another segment of believers claims that the glowing circles of light that often show up on photographs are angels in the form of "orbs."

With such exotic teachings on the rise, we desperately need some biblical guidelines. If you believe everything you hear these days, angels can be huge, tiny, spherical, male, female, feathered or nonfeathered.

The most respected leaders in every corner of the Church, charismatic and noncharismatic, consistently teach that the Bible is our guidebook for doctrine and practice, and that the early Church's experience in the book of Acts should be a pattern for us. This would direct us to assume that if a spiritual experience is not in the Bible, then it should not be considered normative for us today. When I look at what the New Testament teaches us about angels, and specifically what the book of Acts shows us about them, here's what I find:

- Angels who looked like men told the early disciples that Jesus would return one day (Acts 1:11).
- Angels are actively working behind the scenes to minister to the saints, especially to offer protection (Acts 12:7–11).
- In one case an angel directed Philip where to preach (Acts 8:26).

- Angels sometimes appeared in visions to give instructions, as one did for Cornelius (Acts 10:3, 7, 22).
- An angel came to Paul to strengthen him and to assure him that he would preach to Caesar (Acts 27:23–24).

If we look at Paul's epistles, we find only a few references to angels—and most are actually warnings to the early Church about a wrong emphasis on angels:

- Paul warned the Galatians that false angels can bring deception (Galatians 1:8).
- Paul warned the Corinthians about "angels of light" that are messengers of Satan (2 Corinthians 11:14).
- Paul warned the Colossians about misguided people who worship angels and deceive people with their emphasis on mystical experiences that are rooted in their hyperinflated egos (Colossians 2:18).

The book of Hebrews was written to a group of Christians who were considering going back to Old Covenant worship. In the first chapter the author makes it clear that angels have a lower place in God's economy when compared to Jesus Christ. Many Bible scholars believe the readers of this epistle were being tempted to go back to an Old Covenant paradigm in which angels played a more significant role. The author of Hebrews warns these believers to focus their attention instead on the Son of God, who is more glorious than angels.

We can make some basic assumptions about angels in the New Covenant era:

- **Angels help the church fulfill its mission, and they protect and guide the saints.** Every one of us has probably experienced the activity of angels in our lives—often without knowing it because they are usually invisible.
- **Angels sometimes intervene with directive messages.** But there is no case in the New Testament church in which an angel gave his name or brought attention to himself.

- **Angels don't teach or explain doctrine.** In our movement today, some leaders have suggested that certain angels have arrived to usher in new movements. Todd Bentley and others have described his "Emma" as a "nurturing angel" who brings a prophetic movement. But nowhere does the Bible suggest that angels bring moves of God. Jesus commissioned the Church to advance the Kingdom by preaching the Gospel. Angels know this and are expecting us to do our job.

- **Angels don't bring healing.** The New Testament church was commissioned to bring healing "through the name of Jesus"; and Jesus was always the focus for anyone who was healed miraculously. The story of the Pool of Siloam falls under the Old Covenant system, since this phenomenon occurred before the ministry of Jesus. And when Jesus came to that pool, He proved to be a better solution to those who waited for the stirring of the waters.

- **Angels look like people, and in every case in Scripture they appeared to be male.** However, in some cases their appearance was frightening because they carry with them the glory of heaven and the fear of God.

- **False angels preach a different gospel.** One of the devil's strategies is to send counterfeit angelic messengers who bring teaching that is contrary to biblical truth.

There are many flaky, weird and foolish concepts being circulated in our movement today that must be corrected. Charismatic churches that tolerate this kind of quirky mysticism are headed for trouble. Either they will self-destruct when church members grow weary of the constant madness, or a segment of the group will ultimately embrace deception and take on cultlike characteristics.

How can we guard against unhealthy mysticism while leaving room for the miraculous power of God? Pentecostal and charismatic groups have grappled with this issue for years.

Since the apostle Paul was well acquainted with his own first-century version of "charismatic chaos," we do well to find the answer to this question in his first letter to the Corinthians, which contains the classic biblical treatise on the gifts of the Holy Spirit. We can derive four basic principles from the New Testament on this subject.

1. Spiritual gifts, properly used, always edify.

Since you are eager to have spiritual gifts, try to excel in gifts that build up the church.

1 Corinthians 14:12, NIV

True biblical prophecy, as reflected in the New Testament, has little to do with conjecture about the future, wars and rumors of wars, Armageddon or the next stock market crash. It may at times involve the foretelling of a future event, as when the prophet Agabus warned the church at Antioch of a coming famine (Acts 11:28). But such foretelling must always be for the purpose of edification, not to satisfy a base human desire for sensationalism. Too much of the so-called prophesying that goes on in charismatic churches today is a corruption of the real thing.

True prophecy is a message carrying the mark of God on it. It may come in the form of a sermon, but not all sermons can be classified as prophecies since not all preachers seek God earnestly for His message. It may come in the form of an utterance delivered by a church member during a worship service, but not all so-called prophecies given in charismatic services bear the mark of God on them, either.

Paul tells us that all true prophecy must edify. It must stir the Church, not by human emotion or manipulation but by the anointing of the Spirit.

When a so-called prophet's message draws more attention to his own spirituality than to Jesus Christ and His purposes, we can be sure he is not employing the gift of the Holy Spirit. Such a man is exercising his own vanity, trying to impress people by making them think he has a privileged connection to God.

144

2. False prophets are motivated by spiritual pride.

Did the word of God originate with you? . . . If anybody
thinks he is a prophet or spiritually gifted, let him acknowledge that what I am writing to you is the Lord's command.

1 Corinthians 14:36–37, NIV

Paul told the Corinthians that prophets were to be subject
to other prophets. In other words, he was reminding them that
they were not a law unto themselves, spiritual Lone Rangers
inventing their own doctrines. They were to submit themselves to one another in humility, while holding each other
accountable to adhere to the faith.

In Paul's day, the philosophy of gnosticism represented a
major threat to the Church. Gnostics believed that salvation
could be obtained by tapping into a secret source of divine
knowledge reserved for an elite few. To this day the same concept is promoted in charismatic churches. Some charismatic
leaders boast of their discovery of "new" revelations that other
Christians have not recognized. Whole churches sometimes
adopt attitudes of superiority because they have embraced
obscure doctrines about baptism, spiritual warfare or methods
of prayer. They assume that their remarkable knowledge has
set them on a higher plane than ordinary Christians.

But Paul warns us not to be misled by those who claim access to special revelation. In Colossians 2:18–19, he says that
those who make such arrogant boasts have lost connection
with the Head of the Church, the Lord Jesus Christ. There
is no mysterious body of spiritual knowledge waiting to be
revealed. God has unveiled His glorious purpose in His Son,
and our salvation comes from faith in Him alone.

3. God is not the author of confusion.

Therefore, my brothers, be eager to prophesy, and do not
forbid speaking in tongues. But everything should be done
in a fitting and orderly way.

1 Corinthians 14:39–40, NIV

I was in a service once that involved congregations from several area churches in northern Virginia. Following a time of worship, a woman near the front of the auditorium began prophesying in a belligerent tone, condemning the congregation for our "disobedience" and peppering her message with "Thus says the Lord." Her words did not edify, nor was the message prophetic, because it did not reflect the heart of God or offer any redemption.

A blanket of confusion and gloom dropped onto the congregation. People fidgeted anxiously in their seats. This woman claimed to speak for God but her words did not sound like the loving heavenly Father they all knew. If there were non-Christians in the meeting, they probably would have inferred that God was indeed a cruel taskmaster.

Thankfully, one of the local pastors attending the service approached the podium and corrected the woman in a gracious spirit. When he announced that her message was not a true word from God, I could feel everyone in the room breathe a palpable sigh of relief. In a split second, the uneasiness vanished. We all left the meeting that night reassured of God's love—not that God does not chasten His children through His servants the prophets, but that He does not scold us out of frustration or correct us without offering any hope.

False prophecies, regrettably, are not always corrected from the pulpit. Congregations subjected continually to this kind of confusion become prey for all kinds of spiritual and emotional problems. Pastors, as God-appointed shepherds of the flock, are responsible to protect their churches from such abuse.

4. More important than charismatic gifts is the fruit of the Spirit.

If I speak in the tongues of men and of angels, but have not love, I am only a resounding gong or a clanging cymbal.

1 Corinthians 13:1, NIV

Certain Pentecostals and charismatics maintain a profound interest in securing spiritual power. Prophets promise to train Christians how to discern the future. Evangelists offer instruction in how to heal the sick. Some advertise their prowess in casting out demons, while others boast of having mastered the techniques of spiritual warfare over cities and nations.

Certainly we are exhorted in the Scriptures to desire spiritual gifts. But we have need for caution. Our main priority must be to manifest the nature of Christ to the world—not only by doing His works, but by showing His love.

It is time for all of us charismatics and Pentecostals to inspect what we have built over the last few decades. We must determine whether Christian character is the mark of our ministry and ask ourselves if love is at the heart of what we do. Our structures may be impressive and our numbers swelling. But it is possible we are simply making noise with gongs and cymbals, standing on a foundation of sand that can be washed away at any moment.

If we seek to demonstrate to the world the fruit of the Spirit, we can avoid that fate.

Questions for Discussion

1. If Satan can work his own form of miracles, how can we discern the difference between his work and God's work (1 Corinthians 12:8–10)?
2. Why is it important for spiritual leaders to guard the church from false teachers, false prophets and false miracles?
3. In a case such as the Lakeland Revival, what safeguards could have been put into place that would have protected people from deception or spiritual abuse?
4. How can a preoccupation with angels lead to deception?
5. How can we encourage the operation of the miraculous gifts of the Holy Spirit while at the same time guard ourselves from spiritual pride?

The Spirit of the Lord GOD is upon me, because the LORD has anointed me to bring good news to the afflicted; He has sent me to bind up the brokenhearted, to proclaim liberty to captives and freedom to prisoners; to proclaim the favorable year of the LORD and the day of vengeance of our God; to comfort all who mourn.

Isaiah 61:1–2

There is no improving the future without disturbing the present.

Catherine Booth, cofounder of the Salvation Army[1]

Cannot the love of Christ carry the missionary where the slave-trade carries the trader? I shall open up a path to the interior or perish.

David Livingstone, Scottish missionary, doctor and explorer (1813–1873)[2]

What are the shameful, disgraceful things that are happening in the Church of Jesus Christ today? First of all it is the rotten seed that is being preached by covetous shepherds. This is known as the prosperity gospel. This is one of the greatest reproaches that the Church of Jesus Christ ever perpetrated. This perverted gospel is poisoning multitudes—even in China, Africa and all over the world. It is an American gospel invented and spread by rich American evangelists and pastors. It alarms me that so many people can hear the tapes and see videos that are coming out of these prosperity conferences and not weep over them. This poison has spread all over the world.

David Wilkerson[3]

8

The Fire of Justice

The Deonar garbage dump in Mumbai, India, is certainly not a glamorous location for a movie. The first thing that hit me was the smell—an awful combination of urine, rotting food and toxic fumes. But what made me nauseous was watching dozens of skinny Indian children forage through the mountainous heaps of trash looking for their next meal.

Welcome to Mumbai, a city of 24 million made famous in 2008 by Danny Boyle's Oscar-winning film, *Slumdog Millionaire*. The lead character in the movie, a boy named Jamal, grows up near the vast garbage dump (reportedly the world's largest), watches his mother die and then is coerced by a mafia boss into begging for rupees with other love-starved orphans.

If you are wondering whether the film was an accurate portrayal of the poorest kids in India, ask Biju Thampy, a 37-year-old evangelist from southern India who moved to Mumbai in 2006 with his wife, Secunda. They came to the city after hearing about a child in the slums who was drinking milk from a dog. Nowadays Biju and his Vision Rescue

149

team drive two school buses into the Deonar dump to feed eight hundred kids six days a week.

"I used to ask God why people suffer like this," Biju told me as we drove through the narrow dirt roads next to rickety, one-room houses made of tin and scrap wood. "Finally, I came to the place where I stopped asking questions and started being the answer."

With his education and excellent English, Biju could be making lots of money in India or anywhere in the West. But after seeing the needs in the slum, his heart broke. Proverbs 24:11 is one of his life verses: "Deliver those who are being taken away to death, and those who are staggering to slaughter, oh hold them back." As *Slumdog Millionaire* proved, images of poverty can be powerful. I asked Biju what he had seen in the slums of Mumbai that moved him to action. He quickly rattled off a list: (1) He often sees children walking in open drains full of sewage. They have no access to health care. (2) He once saw a sick woman lying on a sidewalk. She had been thrown out of her small slum house because of her illness. (3) He also saw a boy lying dead in a road after he was run over by a bulldozer.

"Life here feels very undignified," he told me.

Biju once led an abused, AIDS-infected prostitute to Christ. The girl owed money to her pimp, so Biju asked him how much it would cost to free her. The answer was $18. Biju paid the money, and the girl spent her final years serving Jesus before succumbing to AIDS.

Biju also sometimes sees children without hands or eyes— and he knows some have been maimed on purpose, just like the boy in *Slumdog Millionaire* who was blinded with acid by his "owners." "Some parents also send these disabled children out in the streets to beg," he told me.

When I visited Deonar on Biju's Vision Rescue bus, I watched as about forty children learned to write simple Hindi phrases on chalkboards. These kids get some simple education and Bible lessons before they are fed a hot lunch of rice and vegetables. Once a week they also get eggs, bread and milk. I prayed with the children and then looked outside the bus to see dozens more waiting their turn.

Biju feeds hundreds of children a week, but there are millions of children in the slum surrounding the Deonar dump. I wondered if that was discouraging, but Biju lit up as he told me about a six-year-old boy named Raj who was rescued two years earlier.

"He was skin and bones, and he had run away from home because his father killed his mother and was beating him," Biju said. "He had a wound on his head. He came up and asked me, 'Can I go with you?'"

Biju was able to take Raj to the city of Goa, where Biju's sister Beena runs a children's home. When Biju visited there recently, Raj told him that he wants to be a pastor when he grows up. "That makes it all worth it," Biju says. "What keeps me going is knowing that one child at a time is being saved."

Biju teaches all the young people on his team to care—not for the crowds, but for the one. "God is leading us these days to focus on the one sheep that is lost, and on the one lost coin. Jesus cares about the one."

I meet Christians like Biju Thampy all over the world. Their hearts are stirred by God for the welfare of the poor and homeless, for drug addicts and prostitutes, for isolated tribes and abused children. They dared to go to the harvest—in Asia, in Africa, in the troubled ghettos of the United States—and there they met the Lord of the harvest. He gave them a holy love for people that compelled them to risk their lives and sacrifice their careers for a cause much bigger than themselves.

God has gripped my own heart in this way on several occasions. It happened when I spent a week with persecuted Christians in China, all of whom had been in jail for their faith three or four times each. It happened when I prayed for sick children in a remote village in eastern Guatemala. It happened when I held AIDS-infected babies at a child rescue center in South Africa.

And it happened again in February 2009 at the Deonar dump, when I looked into the eyes of the skinny children who rummaged through mountains of garbage each morning to find their breakfast. After the 21-hour journey home from India, I could not get those children's faces out of my mind. My heart was breaking. I knew I had to do something to help meet the needs of this desperate world that Jesus came to save.

This is the call of every Christian. If we dare to get close enough to the harvest, we will begin to feel God's burden for the lost and dying. God will ruin us. We will not be able to live "normal" lives again. We will feel compelled to speak on behalf of the downtrodden. This burden is not just reserved for full-time missionaries. Every Christian has a place in the fields of the Lord. We are each called to love the unloved, feed the hungry, protect the vulnerable, heal the abused and cry out for justice for the oppressed.

We Owe the World an Apology

There was a time when the United States seemed to be the headquarters for global missions. We had experienced not one but two Great Awakenings. We provided the birthplace for the modern Pentecostal movement. We sent the largest number of missionaries to the foreign field and we gave the most money to fund global evangelism. That is surely a reason God blessed America with prosperity, technological progress and political freedom.

But something tragic happened in this last generation as American Christianity grew cold and our society became more secular. God's people became selfish. We developed a distorted perspective on money. We invented ear-tickling doctrines that told us God wanted to reward us with luxury cars, three-car garages and Botox treatments. We bought into a self-centered prosperity gospel that poisoned our faith and dampened our missionary zeal.

During my years as editor of *Charisma* I have witnessed a striking contrast between church leaders in America and their counterparts overseas. I visited northern Nigeria, where I interviewed pastors who were forced to watch members of their churches be hacked to death with machetes by Islamic mobs. I spent time with a Peruvian pastor who lives in a tiny house with his family but feeds an entire village. I met Indonesian Christians who risk their lives every day to preach the Gospel in dangerous areas where Muslims sometimes behead Christians.

Then, when I come home from these trips, I turn on a Christian television program and I hear what sounds like a message from another planet. We don't talk about sacrifice. We know nothing of conviction. We shun the cross. Instead, we offer a trite, shallow "bless me" gospel: how to be successful, how to feel better about yourself, how to get your financial breakthrough. Instead of self-denial, we offer self-gratification.

A few years ago, I began apologizing publicly to church leaders overseas for this money-focused gospel we Americans have marketed to the world. During a summit of pastors held in Amsterdam in 2003, I discovered that high-profile Christian speakers from the United States had worn out their welcome because of questionable financial practices and inappropriate demands.

One of Holland's most respected charismatic pastors told me that some American ministers are no longer welcome in his country. "These pastors come here and insist that they must take their own offerings," he told me. "Then they get up in the pulpit and tell the people that if they will give $1,000 each, all will be well and they will be blessed."

Weary of what he considers financial manipulation, this pastor now has a new policy: If a visiting minister insists on taking his own offering, he is not welcome to preach.

A Dutch businessman told me many more horror stories about his dealings with American preachers. Their behavior outside the pulpit, he said, is as disturbing as some of their questionable public demands for donations. Some visiting preachers insisted on pricey hotel rooms—including, on one occasion, a $1,000-a-night penthouse. Others made rude demands of hotel staff. "Many Dutch people look up to these men because they see them on Christian television," the businessman said. "If they knew what went on behind the scenes they would lose all respect for them."

On one occasion an American preacher who was speaking at a Dutch conference was asked if he would come to another city and address a group of pastors. The evangelist asked how much he would be paid for the ministry session. When he was told he would receive $1,000, he looked down at his shoes and said: 'One of my shoes costs more than that. I will not go.'"

When I stood before this group in Holland I had no choice but to extend an olive branch to my wounded brothers and sisters. I shed a few tears as I asked them to forgive us for taking financial advantage of their people. And I prayed publicly that God would cleanse Dutch churches of the pride we had exported to them.

Making that apology was a first step. Now I can only pray that those of us who have misused our place of international influence will find the grace to model a humble and sacrificial lifestyle before it is too late—for God will not tolerate this sick, haughty spirit for long. If we don't repent, plenty of men and women from other parts of the world are capable of stepping into our shoes to provide Christlike leadership. And they will not need to wear $2,500 Italian-leather Oxfords to do the job.

The Profiteers of God

Back in 1992 Hollywood released a feature film about a religious con artist named Jonas Nightingale. The movie, *Leap of Faith*, starred comedian Steve Martin as the cunning preacher who knew how to manipulate Christians in order to get at their wallets. He was the stereotypical huckster, better at preying than praying. The Rev. Nightingale staged an old-fashioned tent revival in a Kansas town, advertised his meetings all over the county and wowed his Pentecostal audiences every night with his miraculous ability to identify people suffering from specific ailments.

Behind the stage Nightingale had an assistant who sent him messages through a tiny electronic earphone. The preacher was not receiving divine messages from God, nor was he healing anyone, but he knew how to create the illusion that lame people could walk. The people were convinced Jonas Nightingale was an anointed man of God. And every night the townsfolk who attended his "revival" services stuffed the offering buckets with what the evangelist was really after: lots of cash.

There will always be Jonas Nightingales for us to watch out for, but most of the corruption and trickery going on in charismatic churches today is far more subtle than the Hollywood version. In actuality, the leaders who are best at manipulating audiences and collecting big offerings are not the outsiders who blow into town with dark sunglasses and criminal records. They are trusted men and women of God who have been enticed over the years by greed.

When Jim Bakker started his broadcast ministry in the early 1960s, he wanted (like many zealous preachers) to reach the world for Christ. But apparently he allowed himself to be deceived by a lust for riches. Years later, after he had spent many months in federal prison for defrauding his followers, he wrote a letter from his cell, which his daughter mailed to his supporters in June 1992. It included this confession:

> Many today believe that the evidence of God's blessing on them is a new car, a new house, a good job, and riches, etc. But that is far from the truth of God's Word. If that be the

155

case, then gambling casino owners and drug kingpins and movie stars are blessed of God. Jesus did not teach that riches were a sign of God's blessings. In fact, Jesus said, "It is hard for a rich man to enter the kingdom of Heaven." And he talked about the "deceitfulness of riches."

I have spent many months reading every word Jesus spoke. I wrote them out over and over, and I read them over and over again. There is no way, if you take the whole counsel of God's Word, that you can equate riches or material things as a sign of God's blessing.

Jesus said, "Blessed are the poor in spirit (humble), blessed are those who mourn, who are meek, who hunger and thirst for righteousness. Blessed are the merciful, the pure in heart, the peacemakers, those who are persecuted, reviled, and spoken of falsely for Christ's sake."

I have asked God to forgive me and I ask all who have sat under my ministry to forgive me for preaching a gospel emphasizing earthly prosperity. Jesus said, "Do not lay up for yourselves treasures on earth." He wants us to be in love with Him. . . . If we equate earthly possessions and earthly relationships with God's favor, what do we tell the billions of those living in poverty, or what do you do if depression hits, or what do you say to those who lose a loved one?[4]

Since Bakker was sentenced to a lengthy prison term, other prominent leaders have distanced themselves from the prosperity message. In 1993 healing evangelist Benny Hinn stunned some of his followers when he announced that he was washing his hands of the so-called prosperity gospel. Hinn told his church, Orlando Christian Center, as well as *Charisma* magazine and a Trinity Broadcasting Network audience, that he no longer believed the message was from God.

What convinced him? Hinn said he came to the conclusion while he was conducting healing crusades in Asia. God would not permit him, he said, to stand before the poverty-stricken people of Manila and promise them that if they gave in the offering, God would bless them with more money. If the prosperity message should not be preached in the Philippines, Hinn decided, it should not be preached in America. "It is not a message from God," he said.

The saddest part of this story is that it took this long for many of us to realize the true origins of this gospel of greed.

Kenneth Hagin's Forgotten Warning

Charismatic Bible teacher Kenneth Hagin Sr. is considered by many to be the father of the prosperity gospel. The folksy, self-trained "Dad Hagin" started a grass-roots movement in Oklahoma that produced a Bible college and a crop of famous preachers including Kenneth Copeland, Jerry Savelle, Charles Capps, Jesse DuPlantis, Creflo Dollar and dozens of others—all of whom teach that Christians who give generously should expect financial rewards on this side of heaven.

Hagin taught that God was not glorified by poverty and that preachers do not have to be poor. But before he died in 2003 and left his Rhema Bible Training Center in the hands of his son, Kenneth Hagin Jr., he summoned many of his colleagues to Tulsa to rebuke them for distorting his message. He was not happy that some of his followers were manipulating the Bible to support what he viewed as greed and selfish indulgence.

Those who were close to Hagin Sr. say he was passionate about correcting these abuses before he died. In fact, he wrote a brutally honest book to address his concerns. *The Midas Touch* was published in 2000, a year after the Tulsa meeting. Many ministers in what is called the Word-Faith Movement sparked by Hagin ignored his book. But in light of the recent controversy over prosperity doctrines it would be a good idea to dust it off and read it again. Here are a few of the points Hagin made in *The Midas Touch*:

- **Financial prosperity is not a sign of God's blessing.** Hagin wrote: "If wealth alone were a sign of spirituality, then drug traffickers and crime bosses would be spiritual giants. Material wealth can be connected to the blessings of God or it can be totally disconnected from the blessings of God."

- **People should never give in order to get.** Hagin was critical of those who "try to make the offering plate some kind of heavenly vending machine." He denounced those who link giving to getting, especially those who give cars to get new cars or who give suits to get new suits. He wrote: "There is no spiritual formula to sow a Ford and reap a Mercedes."

- **It is not biblical to "name your seed" in an offering.** Hagin was horrified by this practice, which was popularized in faith conferences during the 1980s. Faith preachers sometimes tell donors that when they give an offering, they should claim a specific benefit to get a blessing in return. Hagin rejected this idea and said that focusing on what you are going to receive "corrupts the very attitude of our giving nature."

- **The "hundredfold return" is not a biblical concept.** Hagin did the math and figured out that if this bizarre notion were true, "we would have Christians walking around with not billions or trillions of dollars, but quadrillions of dollars!" He rejected the popular teaching that a believer should claim a specific monetary payback rate.

- **Preachers who claim to have a "debt-breaking" anointing should not be trusted.** Hagin was perplexed by ministers who promise "supernatural debt cancellation" to those who give in certain offerings. He wrote in *The Midas Touch*: "There is not one bit of Scripture I know about that validates such a practice. I'm afraid it is simply a scheme to raise money for the preacher, and ultimately it can turn out to be dangerous and destructive for all involved."

Many evangelists who appear on Christian television today use this bogus claim. Usually they insist that the miraculous debt cancellation will occur only if a person "gives right now," as if the anointing for this miracle suddenly evaporates after the prime-time viewing hour. This manipulative claim is more akin to witchcraft than Christian belief.[5]

Hagin condemned other harebrained gimmicks designed to trick audiences into emptying their wallets. He was especially incensed when a preacher told his radio listeners that he would take their prayer requests to Jesus' empty tomb in Jerusalem and pray over them there—if donors included a special love gift. Thanks to the recent resurgence in bizarre donation schemes promoted by American charismatics, the prosperity gospel is back under the nation's microscope. It's time to revisit Hagin's concerns and find a biblical balance.

Hagin told his followers: "Overemphasizing or adding to what the Bible actually teaches invariably does more harm than good." If the man who pioneered the modern concept of biblical prosperity blew the whistle on his own movement, wouldn't it make sense for us to listen to his admonition?

The Deceitfulness of Riches

Kenneth Hagin Sr. and Benny Hinn are not the first charismatic leaders to recognize the inherent flaws in the prosperity gospel. Years before the Jim Bakker–PTL scandal, many believers in America were so repulsed by money-grubbing TV preachers that they returned to their denominational churches in disgust.

It is easy to place blame for this travesty. We could blame the proponents of the prosperity gospel and say it was all caused by faulty theology. But if American church audiences had not already had itching ears eager to embrace the gospel of instant health and wealth, it would never have become such big business in the United States.

The prosperity gospel is not so much a theological problem as it is a heart problem. Those who twist Scripture to say that Jesus was independently wealthy, that His disciples had a condominium in Capernaum or that God owes you a Mercedes-Benz are simply trying to justify their own covetousness. Rather than try to adjust their faulty theology, we should simply recognize that these men are corrupt and we should reject their message, lest we too be tricked by the deccitfulness of riches.

As we charismatics attempt to get our own house in order, I hope we will remove all traces of this corruption. We cannot be a people of biblical justice, or show genuine care for the poor, if we promote these doctrines of greed. How can we be sure the love of money is not defiling our churches and ministries? Here are three danger signals that can alert us to the presence of a charlatan.

1. Beware of shepherds who do not feed their sheep.

Covetous people care for no one but themselves. When the deceitfulness of riches grips a person's heart, it prevents him or her from caring for others or expressing genuine compassion. This is why the Bible says that a church leader who loves money is disqualified from serving the people of God (1 Timothy 3:3). His heart cannot possibly be a channel of God's love.

A pastor I know of was often asked to travel to various cities during the week to preach in special crusades. A dynamic speaker, he got lots of these invitations. Every time he preached, the church handed him an honorarium check, sometimes in excess of $3,000 or $4,000. In some cases they also handed him a wad of cash that had been put into the offering plate after the check had been written.

This evangelist often took the cash and headed to his favorite men's clothing shop. He admitted to his closest associates that he had a special affection for nice things, and he was known to spend up to $400 on belts and ties during one shopping spree. He spent many times that amount on gold and diamond jewelry.

Is this where money from a church offering plate belongs? Certainly ministers deserve to be supported generously for their services. But we don't need a supernatural gift of discernment to determine whether a man or woman of God has crossed the line into materialistic excess. If Christians would stop defending ministers who lead such lifestyles, we might see a return to biblical holiness among our church leaders who continue to invite and support them.

The Lord sent a stern rebuke through the prophet Ezekiel to spiritual leaders who insist on fleecing the flock for their own benefit. Though it was directed at the Jewish priests of apostate Israel, it applies to any contemporary pastor or evangelist who aims to get rich off of the people of God:

> Son of man, prophesy against the shepherds of Israel; prophesy and say to them: "This is what the Sovereign LORD says: Woe to the shepherds of Israel who only take care of themselves! Should not shepherds take care of the flock? You eat the curds, clothe yourselves with the wool and slaughter the choice animals, but you do not take care of the flock. You have not strengthened the weak or healed the sick or bound up the injured. You have not brought back the strays or searched for the lost. You have ruled them harshly and brutally. So they were scattered because there was no shepherd, and when they were scattered they became food for all the wild animals. . . .
>
> "This is what the Sovereign LORD says: I am against the shepherds and will hold them accountable for my flock. I will remove them from tending the flock so that the shepherds can no longer feed themselves. I will rescue my flock from their mouths, and it will no longer be food for them."
>
> Ezekiel 34:2–5, 10, NIV

God clearly has strong feelings about shepherds who care more for themselves than for the sheep that have been entrusted to their care. We should be just as protective, speaking out when we see a church leader falling into the trap of materialism.

2. Beware of any church leader whose message seems money-centered.

The Bible has plenty to say about money: how to save it, how to spend it, how to invest it, how to give it away. There is a legitimate need for Christians to learn biblical principles of money management, and churches often struggle financially because their members have never learned the biblical basis for tithing.

But the prosperity gospel, at its core, has little to do with biblical principles. Of course, many of the principles taught by the prosperity preachers are sound doctrine. The Bible says clearly, for example, "Give, and it will be given to you. A good measure, pressed down, shaken together and running over, will be poured into your lap. For with the measure you use, it will be measured to you" (Luke 6:38, NIV).

The essence of this passage is obvious: God wants us to be generous. Jesus' instructions are to encourage us to display an attitude of cheerful sharing rather than hold tightly to our worldly possessions. Giving releases us to trust the Father for His abundant provision. But this verse is often manipulated to entice people to put large sums of money into an offering plate or a direct mail envelope. It has even been made into a formula: If you give Amount A and you are using enough faith, God will multiply it into Amount B.

But the prosperity preachers have conveniently left out some of Jesus' other teachings on giving, especially His admonition in Matthew 6:1–4 (NIV):

> Be careful not to do your "acts of righteousness" before men, to be seen by them. If you do, you will have no reward from your Father in heaven.

So when you give to the needy, do not announce it with trumpets, as the hypocrites do in the synagogues and on the streets, to be honored by men. I tell you the truth, they have received their reward in full. But when you give to the needy, do not let your left hand know what your right hand is doing, so that your giving may be in secret.

So much of the giving that occurs in charismatic churches in the name of faith is nothing more than self-congratulatory trumpet-blowing—bragging in public about our sacrifices to God when He says that giving is a holy act to be done in secret. Because we have blown our trumpets so loudly and made money a central part of our message, many worship services resemble boisterous sales rallies. The love of money has tainted our praise. It has caused many of us to shift our focus from the spiritual to the material and assume that all God's blessings are in the material realm.

The devil himself must have engineered this, since he is a master at luring us to focus our attention on the things of the flesh rather than the things of the Spirit. If we were more discerning, we would have noticed early on what a hollow ring the prosperity message produced.

But many of us were deceived by that hollow sound. Today we face the challenge of removing this corruption from our midst and preaching a purified message free from greed and idolatry.

3. Reject those who take the Lord's name in vain.

The third commandment prohibits us from taking the Lord's name in vain. Yet there are evangelists and church leaders who misuse the Lord's name every day when they raise money. One of America's most notorious televangelists spends up to 80 percent of his air time urging his viewers to make "$1,000 vows of faith" to his ministry. He claims that God will rescue his listeners from debt, poverty or failed businesses if they will become obedient givers.

During his syndicated TV program, this evangelist peers into the camera and claims to discern the specific needs of people in his viewing audience. "I see a businessman," the evangelist says. "You're sitting in your hotel room, discouraged about how your business is going. I see a housewife at home. You're so tired of not having enough to pay the bills." Then he explains how the solution works: "Send me your money and God will bless you. Operators are standing by. You can even put the bill on your MasterCard or Visa."

This man has crossed into dangerous territory. He claims to speak for God, sometimes even prophesying in the name of Christ, while his motive is apparent: to entice his listeners to send him their money. Despite the many missions projects this evangelist funds, the whole nation learned about his extravagant lifestyle in 1991 when a national news program investigated his fund-raising methods.

When it comes to how we treat other people's money, we charismatics need a fresh dose of the fear of God. It borders on blasphemy when church leaders stand in the pulpit and say with an air of authority, "God has told me that ten people in the audience are to give $2,000 each," or (even worse), "God is saying that those who give in this offering will receive a hundredfold return." How can we have the audacity to make such presumptuous, manipulative statements?

A list of such gimmicks would be endless. One of the most common is used in direct mail promotions sent by various ministries. In the fund-raising letter, the evangelist asks his supporters to write their prayer requests on a special card, which also includes a place to write in the amount of a designated gift. Somewhere in his letter, the evangelist implies that those who send back their prayer request with money will obtain an instant answer from God.

Is this any different from the medieval practice of buying indulgences from the Catholic Church?

The only way this sad state of affairs can be corrected is for those of us in the pews to demand a higher level of integrity on the part of our leaders. We must demand that the biblical standard be upheld: Greed is grounds for disqualification from church leadership.

What we need today is a holy baptism of justice. We must repent of our selfishness, reject self-centered doctrines and turn away from financial practices that cater to the flesh. And then we must ask God to give us His heart for the poor we are called to serve.

Questions for Discussion

1. Describe a time when you saw real poverty. How did you react?
2. Why do you think the American church has been so susceptible to a shallow gospel that focuses on material things?
3. After reading Kenneth Hagin Sr.'s comments in *The Midas Touch*, can you identify any false notions about money that you have believed?
4. Why is it so important that church leaders be free from the love of money?

It was for freedom that Christ set us free; therefore keep standing firm and do not be subject again to a yoke of slavery.

Galatians 5:1

For the Lord is the Spirit, and wherever the Spirit of the Lord is, there is freedom.

2 Corinthians 3:17, NLT

Accountability, personal training under the guidance of another, and effective pastoral care are needed biblical concepts. True spiritual maturity will require that they be preserved. These biblical realities must also carry the limits indicated by the New Testament. However, to my personal pain and chagrin, these particular emphases very easily lent themselves to an unhealthy submission resulting in perverse and unbiblical obedience to human leaders. Many of these abuses occurred within the sphere of my own responsibility.

Bob Mumford, co-founder of
the Discipleship Movement, in his
1990 public apology for the spiritual
abuse the movement caused[1]

9

The Fire of Spiritual Liberty

When Jorge Serrano Elias was elected president of Guatemala in 1991, he was heralded as the first democratically elected evangelical to head a government in Latin America. His election was seen as a signal that the rapidly growing evangelical population in Guatemala was now large enough to make a major impact in a Catholic-dominated country.

But President Serrano, a Pentecostal who prayed publicly at state events and talked privately about sharing the Gospel with Cuban leader Fidel Castro, proved a disappointment, both to the Christians in Guatemala who elected him and to the evangelical community around the world who had seen him as a trendsetter. In 1993, in an effort to root out corruption, Serrano dissolved the Congress, seized control of the press and rallied the military to support his coup. But Guatemala's Supreme Court condemned his actions, as did the international community. Within a week he was forced to flee the country. Serrano had followed in the footsteps of countless Latin American leaders before him: He had become a dictator.

Why did everyone, including Guatemala's evangelicals, condemn Serrano's seizure of power? Because it is impossible to reconcile Christianity with dictatorship, and Serrano had apparently tried to mix two opposing ideas: democracy and autocratic rule. Christians hope his failure taught his peers that Christian heads of state in developing nations of Africa, Latin America and Asia must leave the power in the hands of the people.

But Serrano's ouster sent another message: Christians can be dictators. Sadly, charismatic churches in the United States have accommodated "Christian dictatorship." Many of our leaders wield absolute power while most of us, unfamiliar with principles of godly church government, neglect to challenge their governing style. And many, many people have been hurt as a result.

The apostle Peter laid down a set of guidelines for church leadership when he wrote his first epistle to the early Church:

> To the elders among you, I appeal as a fellow elder, a witness of Christ's sufferings and one who also will share in the glory to be revealed: Be shepherds of God's flock that is under your care, serving as overseers—not because you must, but because you are willing, as God wants you to be; not greedy for money, but eager to serve; not lording it over those entrusted to you, but being examples to the flock.
>
> 1 Peter 5:1–3, NIV

Heavy-handed leadership is the way of the world. But Peter reminded the believers in Asia Minor that Christ had introduced a revolutionary new approach: leadership through humility, servanthood and example. Jesus demonstrated that radical approach to leadership when He stripped to slave dress in order to wash His disciples' feet. When two of His closest followers entertained a lust for power, Jesus told them,

> You know that the rulers of the Gentiles lord it over them, and their high officials exercise authority over them. Not so

168

with you. Instead, whoever wants to become great among you must be your servant, and whoever wants to be first must be your slave—just as the Son of Man did not come to be served, but to serve, and to give his life as a ransom for many.

Matthew 20:25–28, NIV

This godly method of governing, however, has not been the rule in most charismatic churches. Since the renewal blossomed in the late 1960s, many groups that began with vibrant faith degenerated quickly into legalism and authoritarianism. Some ministry leaders have exalted themselves as kings over their own kingdoms, giving their churches or ministries the characteristics of cults.

Spiritual Abuse and Unhealthy "Submission"

Keith was barely eighteen in 1970 when he got involved in the House of Bread, a charismatic prayer group that met on Saturday nights in a rustic cabin in northern Virginia, just ten miles outside of Washington, D.C. Like many other young people touched by the Jesus Movement, Keith was eager to serve the Lord and give his energies to winning his friends to Christ.

The House of Bread was a healthy place to do that. The worship was rich, the Bible study enlightening and the friendships deep. The prayer group soon became an officially organized church, and at age twenty Keith was recognized as an elder. Jim, an older man with an Assemblies of God background, pastored the church and took Keith under his wing.

But trouble was brewing. In its formative years, the House of Bread became aligned with the Discipleship Movement—a network of charismatic churches that emphasized the need for strict pastoral oversight. Because these men had hammered out a special covenant among themselves, submitting

169

their lives and ministries to one another, they taught that all Christians, in order to grow spiritually, should likewise submit themselves to a personal pastor or "shepherd."

The Shepherding Movement, like many Christian fads, swept through the Church in the 1970s and 1980s and was embraced to varying degrees by many charismatic groups. Critics warned that Scripture does not encourage believers to depend on their pastors or spiritual "overseers" for daily guidance, and the movement was opposed as heresy by a few prominent voices in the Church, including Pat Robertson and Jack Hayford.

But for Keith, the shepherding message seemed biblically sound, and he longed for close-knit covenant relationships. Keith was eager to submit his life to Jim because he had so much to learn. And since Jim tended to be easygoing, Keith knew that Jim would not expect him to come for advice every time he needed to make a personal decision.

Not everyone involved in the Discipleship Movement fared so well. In some churches members were told where they should be employed and what kind of furniture they should buy for their homes. Others were instructed that they needed pastoral approval before they could read certain books or have children!

But Keith became a casualty of the movement after more than a decade when he began to register complaints about how the church was operated. He was paid a generous salary, and two other senior pastors were paid even more, but it bothered Keith that information about the pastors' salaries and benefits was not made available to the congregation. The budget was hidden because the church leaders did not feel the people had a right to know.

After raising questions about this autocratic management style, Keith was labeled a rebel. He resigned. Jim, to whom he had looked for spiritual direction for more than twelve years, announced to the congregation that Keith was "under the influence of Satan."

It took years for Keith and his wife to recover from the emotional devastation they experienced. Part of their healing came when the Discipleship Movement imploded.

In 1989, Bob Mumford, one of the five key leaders of that movement, issued a formal apology to the Body of Christ, repenting for spreading teaching that caused so much abuse. His statement said that the Shepherding Movement had encouraged "an unhealthy submission resulting in perverse and unbiblical obedience to human leaders." Mumford then expressed regret: "Many of these abuses occurred within the spheres of my own responsibility. For the injury and shame caused to people, families and the larger Body of Christ, I repent with sorrow and ask for your forgiveness."[2]

In a subsequent interview with *Ministries Today* editor Jamie Buckingham, Mumford admitted that the shepherding emphasis was heresy. "I now see the biblical warnings, 'Don't lord it over the flock.' But I did. In my own heart, I got this triumphant feeling of being in charge. People, on the other hand, felt handled and pressured. We wrongly gave the impression you could not fellowship with any of us unless you did things our way. And that was wrong."[3]

That same year Maranatha Campus Ministries, a vibrant outreach to college students, disbanded after its leaders recognized their errors relating to authoritarianism. Maranatha's founder, Bob Weiner, issued a public apology. Church members had made inordinate personal sacrifices so that the group could succeed. Some put their careers on hold to support the local church. Others chose to forgo marriage because they feared they might compromise their standards by marrying someone outside the ministry.

Loyalty to the ministry had been reinforced to the point of blacklisting people who left. The demise of Maranatha was fast, but it would take years for some Maranatha disciples to recover from the spiritual abuse they encountered during their years of association with the group.

And while Maranatha leaders orchestrated some significant evangelistic breakthroughs on dozens of university campuses, the ministry left a trail of wounded people. Abuses
ranged from absurd to devastating. Because Maranatha's
young pastors were expected to groom their disciples to look
their best, overweight people were reported to the ministry's
headquarters and their names placed on a list. Several times
a year their pastors were required to report on their weight
loss progress. At one point, the ministry's elders threatened
to excommunicate anyone who refused to get in shape.

Maranatha leaders were skilled in using Scripture to encourage loyalty, and anyone who balked at the idea of "total
commitment" to the group was judged guilty of harboring a
"spirit of rebellion." Anyone brave enough to ask questions
was accused of having a demon of "intellectualism" or "mind
idolatry." Those courageous enough to leave the group were
considered spiritually inferior.

I wish I could say that this form of spiritual control went
out of style in the late 1980s, but abuses continue to this day
in the charismatic movement.

- In the 1990s charismatic leaders began to emphasize
  the need for apostles. Unfortunately, some of the men
  who stepped into this role did not follow the model of
  humility set by Paul and other New Testament church
  fathers. Some charismatic apostles engineered elaborate
  "downlines" so that the leaders under them tithed to
  them. Many of these apostles became quite wealthy.
  Some began to charge a fee for those who wanted to
  become their "spiritual sons."

- Many smaller networks of charismatic churches today
  are controlled by one dominant leader. One group in
  Florida has bylaws stating that the founder cannot be
  questioned. Another group in Arizona has been in tur-
  moil for a decade because of its founder's harsh threats
  and tyrannical demands.

- Often in these churches all control is vested in an "apostolic father"—and the leader even owns the church property. The idea of having a church council, a board of elders or an accountability committee is never considered.

Seven Warning Signs of an Unhealthy Church

The only way we can root out authoritarianism from our churches is by teaching Christians to recognize the difference between godly and ungodly leadership. For too long charismatics have tolerated bad leaders and embraced in turn their flawed philosophy of governing by manipulation. We have encouraged tyranny rather than servanthood in our churches. The spiritual abuse perpetrated by authoritarian leaders in the Church has resulted in thousands upon thousands of wounded believers—people who can no longer trust the Church to be a sanctuary and who no longer expect pastors to be healers.

In 1978 the whole world watched as a large congregation of naïve souls in Jonestown, Guyana, died because they allowed a madman named Jim Jones to control them with his apocalyptic preaching. In 1993 we watched a similar tragic scenario play out when cult leader David Koresh and his band of loyal Branch Davidians holed up in a compound in Waco, Texas, and met their deaths, convinced God was on their side and everyone outside their tiny world was deceived.

After watching such tragic scenes on the evening news, many non-Christians are wary of anyone who teaches from the Bible with an authoritative tone. In some charismatic circles, by contrast, *we* are naïve. We put so much trust in our leaders that some of our churches have become virtual personality cults. In our lack of discernment we leave ourselves vulnerable. Many of us, like sheep eager to be led to greener pastures, exercise insufficient caution about whom we follow.

It is time we challenge authoritarianism and call it what it is: an illegitimate use of God's name and authority. It is time we learn to identify illegitimate authority in our ranks, not just to protect ourselves but to spare our friends and family members the pain of spiritual abuse. It is time we care as much for the flock of God as we do for the reputation of the shepherds. It is time we call for an end to abuse within the walls of our churches.

How can we know when a particular church or church leader is crossing into the danger zone of authoritarianism? Here are seven warning signs I have detected in my own experience.

1. Lack of accountability. The Scriptures tell us there is safety in the multitude of counselors (Proverbs 11:14). It stands to reason, then, that there is much less safety—perhaps even danger—when a leader does not bother to seek counsel from a wide and diverse group of his peers, as well as from gray-haired men and women who have the wisdom that comes with age. If a pastor or church leader is not open to correction from his colleagues, he has set himself up for failure and displayed a blatant form of pride.

Because sex abuse by clergy has become such a prominent problem in our society, more and more congregations are insisting that their leaders become accountable to an intimate support group in which they can confess their sins and discuss personal struggles. A humble church leader will admit he needs such a system of accountability. A proud, authoritarian leader will not admit that need, nor dare make himself vulnerable to people he deems spiritually inferior or a possible threat to his position or authority.

2. Lack of acceptance of other denominations, churches or ministries. The Lone Ranger needs no one to teach him, and his insecurity forces him to compare himself continually to others to prove his superiority. A humble leader, on the other hand, recognizes his limitations and knows he is serving just one function among many in the Body of Christ. Any pastor not in regular fellowship with other Christian leaders in his city is sending a clear message: "I have no need of you."

For many years independent kingdom-building has been a typical and acceptable method for ministry in the United States, but it has proven to produce bad fruit. Kingdom-builders end up trying to grab some of the glory that belongs only to God. Absolute power, as the saying goes, corrupts absolutely. We need to expect our leaders to display an attitude of humility toward the rest of the Body of Christ.

3. An atmosphere of control. Authoritarian leaders know how to control people through manipulation. In some cases, this control may simply take the form of subtle suggestions and persuasion. In the most abusive situations, it is applied as threats, legalistic demands, unreasonable requirements and false doctrines. In some cases, especially in charismatic circles, it can come through witchcraft or other forms of spiritual manipulation, such as misguided prophecies or "words of knowledge."

Authoritarian church leaders are masters at using Scripture to manipulate people. They often quote 1 Chronicles 16:22: "Do not touch My anointed ones, and do My prophets no harm." Another favorite is Hebrews 13:17: "Obey your leaders and submit to their authority. They keep watch over you as men who must give an account" (NIV). Such passages can be used to intimidate people and keep them from challenging wrong. Some pastors don't recognize the legitimate distinction between valid criticism and slander. And some actually declare that God will curse anyone who even criticizes them.

The signs of an oppressive, controlling church environment are apparent. Spiritual heaviness lies like a thick cloud over the congregation, and few believers manifest genuine joy because they are overburdened by feelings of guilt and frustration.

This was the situation with the Galatians. Because these believers had been "bewitched" by Jewish legalists insisting on complicating the Gospel with endless regulations, and because they had begun to follow the dictates of men rather than Christ, Paul told them they had deserted Christ for "a different gospel" (Galatians 1:6, NIV); that they were "trying to attain [their] goal by human effort" (3:3, NIV); that they must want to be "enslaved . . . all over again" (4:9, NIV); and that they had been "alienated from Christ" and had "fallen away from grace" (5:4, NIV).

Paul's prescription for recovery from this spiritual ailment is simple: "Stand firm, then, and do not let yourselves be burdened again by a yoke of slavery" (5:1, NIV). We are responsible to walk in the freedom provided us by Christ and His Gospel. We must oppose legalism and spiritual control in every form, because to allow ourselves to be controlled is to throw away our liberty in Christ.

4. Dominating attitudes in leaders, usually manifested by haughtiness and anger. Tyrants are surprisingly similar. Because they want to control their surroundings, they often blow up when people do not conform to their demands or don't do so as quickly as they wish. We might expect bullying in the corporate world, but we should not tolerate it among church leaders.

Paul did not tolerate it. He wrote that overseers should not be "violent" or "quarrelsome" but "self-controlled" and "gentle" (1 Timothy 3:2–3, NIV). Later he instructed Timothy that the Lord's servant "must not quarrel; instead, he must be kind to everyone" (2 Timothy 2:24, NIV).

The Old Testament has plenty to say on this subject as well. Proverbs 22:24–25, for example, warns, "Do not make friends with a hot-tempered man, do not associate with one easily angered, or you may learn his ways and get yourself ensnared" (NIV).

In 1988 a woman who attended an Assemblies of God church in Texas was summoned to the pulpit by the pastor and told she was a devil. When the woman asked why, the pastor exploded angrily, rushed off the platform and tried to drag her out of the auditorium. One onlooker said the congregation was in shock because they respected the woman for her spirituality.

A few moments later, other members of the church, taking their cue from the pastor, assaulted the woman and prevented her from calling the police. She later reported her plight to a denominational official and months later filed a lawsuit against the church and pastor. In 1990 she was awarded more than $60,000 in damages for physical injury and emotional pain. The woman's attorney told a newspaper reporter that the jury's decision in the case indicated that "free expression of religion doesn't mean you're free to victimize anyone in the name of religion."

It is sad that such behavior by ministers is not only tolerated but in some cases defended by their followers.

5. Emphasis on leaders hearing God for the people, rather than encouraging them to hear God for themselves. The Bible teaches that every believer has direct access to God through one mediator, Jesus Christ. Every Christian, moreover, can hear God's voice personally and expect to receive God's guidance.

In authoritarian church situations, however, members are not encouraged to seek God's guidance themselves. Rather, they are urged to conform to the leader's preferences. In some cases, leaders actually teach their congregations to seek counsel and specific approval from a pastor before making a major decision. Thus, the church members develop an unhealthy dependence on a man in order to function spiritually, and a diminished ability to trust God.

In one charismatic group, pastors encouraged their disciples to check in with them daily to assess their spiritual health and receive any needed guidance. Church members were expected to get approval from their pastors before making major purchases, taking family vacations or planning to have children.

The emotional devastation caused by this kind of perverted control is immeasurable. For many who submitted to the philosophy behind the so-called Shepherding Movement, it took years to recover from the loss of decision-making ability. They relinquished their wills and lost their identities— because they viewed absolute obedience to their spiritual leaders as a Christian virtue.

6. Leaders assuming ownership of their people and churches. Leaders within authoritarian groups operate in a sub-biblical understanding of spiritual authority. Rather than see their role as that of a servant to encourage, strengthen and equip the people of God, authoritarian leaders inflate their own importance and view themselves as somehow "owning" the people God has entrusted to them for spiritual oversight.

In the churches associated with the Discipleship Movement, for example, it was common for a leader to refer to "his men," meaning the ten or twelve men he was shepherding. This mentality led some leaders to require (though it is hard to believe) that "their men" actually tithe their income directly to them rather than to a church offering account.

Ownership of the people led to the next step: ownership of the people's resources. In authoritarian environments, pastors often gather to themselves a tightly controlled band of elders (sometimes relatives) to set governmental and financial policies. The church is governed, once again, like a dictatorship, and the congregation has little input into church programs. Pastors' salaries remain undisclosed, and the pastor maintains control of the church board, if there is one. It is, in essence, a form of feudalism that is still accepted by Christians in the twenty-first century.

Such a system is a far cry from the biblical view of the church as a living organism, kept vibrant as each member plays a part. All church members should share a sense of ownership in the local church, while realizing that only Christ is the owner of His Kingdom.

7. Women viewed as inferior. Churches and denominations in America diverge greatly in their view of women in leadership. Some permit the ordination of women, even as senior pastors or bishops, while others maintain that Scripture does not permit women to exercise authority over men in ministry settings.

Apart from these differences of opinion on biblical interpretation, it should be noted that authoritarian churches or groups usually discourage women from pursuing any genuine role in ministry. In most of them, women are viewed as important only in their functions as wives and mothers, and they are not encouraged to step beyond these confines to pursue ministry opportunities.

This view creates nothing but frustration, of course. And such a low view leads men to treat women as God-ordained sex objects or drones equipped to perform only menial tasks. Women eager to be used by God or to share their spiritual insights with church leaders are branded rebels or "Jezebels."

The Church was intended to be a place of refuge for the redeemed community, not a place to be browbeaten and abused. How tragic that many of the lambs God has gently prodded into churches associated with the gifts of the Spirit have not found there the loving care of the Great Shepherd.

May God give us a fresh baptism of the Spirit of liberty so our churches can be healthy and our pastors and leaders will reflect the heart of the Great Shepherd.

Questions for Discussion

1. Why is it important for church leaders to have some system of accountability?
2. How should a person respond if he or she is in a church that has unhealthy control or manipulation?
3. Read the qualifications of a church overseer in 1 Timothy 3:2–7. What specific qualifications in this passage would disqualify an abusive, domineering leader?

In the same way the Spirit also helps our weakness; for we do not know how to pray as we should, but the Spirit Himself intercedes for us with groanings too deep for words; and He who searches the hearts knows what the mind of the Spirit is, because He intercedes for the saints according to the will of God.

Romans 8:26–27

How little time the average Christian spends in prayer! We are too busy to pray, and so we are too busy to have power. We have a great deal of activity, but we accomplish little; there are many services, but few conversions. The power of God is lacking in our lives and in our work. We have not because we ask not.

R. A. Torrey[1]

Prayer is the greatest power God has put into our hands for service—praying is harder than doing, at least I find it so, but the dynamic lies that way to advance the Kingdom.

Mary Slessor, Scottish missionary who spent her life in West Africa (1848–1915)[2]

So we come to one of the crying evils of our times, maybe of all times—little or no praying. Of these two evils, perhaps little praying is worse than no praying. Little praying is kind of make-believe, a salve for the conscience, a farce and a delusion.

E. M. Bounds, *Power Through Prayer*[3]

10

The Fire of Prayer

In the summer of 1976, when I was preparing to enter my first semester in college, I learned that the woman teaching my Sunday school class was a "charismatic." I didn't know what that term meant. It sounded to me like some kind of back problem!

I had never heard the term glossolalia, either. It, too, sounded like a horrible disease. I was a Southern Baptist teenager who had never been in any type of Pentecostal meeting. But June Leverette had my attention that day when she began her lesson from the gospel of John.

"If any man is thirsty, let him come to Me and drink," she read in the tranquil drawl of a Georgia native.

I had probably heard that verse a few times. But somehow that morning it was amplified. I could hear in June's words the voice of the Lord calling me to Himself.

I was already a Christian. I had attended Southern Baptist churches since my childhood, made public profession of my faith several times and was a regular in my youth group. But when June read that passage from John 7 on this particular morning, a light went on inside me. I suddenly understood that Christianity was much, much more than Bible verses and church programs and Sunday services and senior high retreats.

I sensed that this Jesus Christ I had claimed to know for several years was calling me to know Him in a deeper way. I had never felt His call so strongly.

Yet I had no idea how to respond. And I was full of questions: *Is my Christian experience missing something? What else does Jesus have to offer me besides salvation? Is there more to the Christian life than just struggling to overcome temptation? Are the words of the Bible relevant for me today?*

"If any man is thirsty, let him come to Me and drink," June read again.

There was something unusual about June Leverette. She talked about Jesus as if she had just had a conversation with Him in the car on her way to church. She seemed to exude joy and peace and love. She talked about prayer as if it were something adventurous and exciting. When she read the Bible aloud, it seemed to come alive. I didn't know her well, but it was obvious she was the kind of person who could share her faith confidently with others. That was something I wished I could do, but the thought of witnessing to strangers mortified me.

"He who believes in Me, as the Scripture said, 'From his innermost being shall flow rivers of living water,'" June read. Then she proceeded to talk about the Holy Spirit.

The Holy Spirit gives us power to be witnesses, she explained. The Holy Spirit enlightens us to know God's will and helps us live in a way that is pleasing to the Father. The Holy Spirit wants to fill us and channel the flow of God's love and power to others. The Holy Spirit is our Teacher, our Guide, our Comforter.

It was obvious to me that June had encountered the Holy Spirit *personally*. Then another light went on inside me. In all my years of church activities, this was the first time I remembered hearing someone teach about the Person or work of the Holy Spirit. As June Leverette began to describe how the Holy Spirit had become real to her in recent days, I hung on her words.

When the 39-minute lesson was over, I knew I wanted what June had, whatever that was. I had no idea what a charismatic or Pentecostal was. I knew nothing about the *charismata*, or gifts of the Holy Spirit, and no one I knew had ever addressed the issue of speaking in tongues. Healing was not discussed, either. Whenever we prayed for the sick during church services, we usually asked God to comfort the people on the hospital visitation list.

And so I naïvely asked June, in a conversation at her house not long afterward, to explain to me why no pastor of any church I had attended had ever discussed this so-called baptism in the Holy Spirit she was advocating. (I later learned that she invited me to her home because our pastor had asked her not to talk about her charismatic experience at the church!) She told me, in her gracious Southern way, that anyone, whether a pastor or a teenager like me, could be filled with the Holy Spirit's power. That settled it for me. I wanted to take the plunge.

June loaded me down with books, including one titled, *Why Should I Speak in Tongues?* I knew it wasn't a Baptist book, but this Baptist Sunday school teacher said it changed her life. So I figured it was safe.

After reading the books and several Bible passages on the subject, I discovered that many people in the book of Acts spoke in tongues (for which the Greek is *glossolalia*). Even the apostle Paul did! And he boasted to the Corinthians: "I thank God that I speak in tongues more than all of you" (1 Corinthians 14:18, NIV). Once I became convinced that this was a biblical experience, I sat on a volleyball court outside my church in suburban Atlanta and looked up at the night sky.

I was hungry for more of God. I prayed a simple prayer: "Lord, I'm Yours, and I want all You have for me. Fill me with Your Spirit." Then I cringed. I didn't know what to expect. It was a dangerous prayer!

I didn't hear the sound of a rushing wind. There were no claps of thunder, and no flames of Pentecostal fire. But the next day when I was in my room praying, I could tell that a heavenly language was bubbling up inside me. I opened my mouth and the words spilled out. *Ilia skiridan tola do skan tama.* Or something like that.

I had no clue what I was saying. It sounded like gibberish. Yet when I prayed in tongues I felt close to God. And when I read about the phenomenon of "praying in the Spirit" in the New Testament, I learned it is a precious spiritual gift that edifies the believer.

My relationship with God was energized, and I've been praying in tongues ever since. And I've met hundreds of people from all over the world who pray in the Spirit every day, including hairstylists, politicians, migrant farm workers, doctors, lawyers, waitresses, professors, professional athletes, celebrity musicians, cab drivers and wealthy businesspeople. And lots of Southern Baptist pastors!

You could say this makes me a "Bapticostal." I don't wear denominational labels, and I don't attend a Baptist church today, but my Baptist roots go so deep you couldn't pull them up with a bulldozer. I may act like a Pentecostal when I raise my hands, dance or shout hallelujah, but if you cut me open you'll see Baptist blood. It runs thick in my family.

Some people think "Baptist" and "Pentecostal" are opposites, so to them the thought of matching the two is like pairing a hippopotamus with a hyena. I don't see it that way. I never would have been drawn into a Pentecostal experience if I hadn't been taught by Baptists to read the Bible for myself. Baptists taught me that if the Bible says it, I should believe it. So when I read that Christians in the early Church spoke in ecstatic, unknown languages, I believed I could too.

This is why I was so troubled by what happened in 2006 at Southwestern Baptist Theological Seminary, the premier theological institution of the Southern Baptist Convention (SBC). A visiting Baptist minister, Dwight McKissic—who served on the seminary's board of trustees—told students at a late summer chapel service that he speaks in tongues in his "private prayer life."

McKissic, pastor of Cornerstone Baptist Church in Arlington, Texas, told the audience at the Fort Worth seminary: "Not all Baptists believe that the gift of tongues went out with the completion of the New Testament. Some of the foremost thinkers and leaders and theologians among Baptist life believe tongues is a valid gift for today."[4]

McKissic did not give a demonstration of his glossolalia, but he testified that he was baptized in the Holy Spirit in 1981 while a student at Southwestern. Said McKissic: "I didn't even believe in speaking in tongues. I was just going through my regular prayer time. As I was praying some strange words began to come out of my mouth."[5]

Just like me, he was zapped by God on Baptist property!

McKissic also criticized the SBC's International Mission Board for its policy forbidding Southern Baptist missionaries who speak in tongues from serving on the field. "I think it's tragic in Baptist life when we take a valid gift that the Bible talks about and come up with a policy that says people who pray in tongues in their private prayer lives cannot work in certain positions," the pastor said.

Concerned that more seminary students might become Bapticostals as a result of McKissic's message, Southwestern's president, Paige Patterson, officially rebuked McKissic and announced that his offending sermon would not be available on the school's website. Some observers accused Patterson and the seminary of religious censorship. Others debated whether speaking in tongues should be "normative" in Baptist churches.

The controversy made me wonder: Shouldn't we be more concerned with what is normative in the New Testament church than with maintaining a religious status quo? Is Jesus going to measure our spiritual fruit by a biblical standard or by a Baptist standard?

Baptists taught me from childhood that the Bible is the inerrant Word of God. And my Bible says, "Do not forbid to speak in tongues" (1 Corinthians 14:39). So why are Baptist leaders forbidding and censoring what the Bible promotes? Are they afraid that the Holy Spirit, who cannot be controlled by committees or religious policies, will misbehave?

I know hundreds of Southern Baptists—including many in prominent leadership positions—who have experienced Pentecost. They pray in tongues in their personal devotional time. They also believe in healing, spiritual warfare, casting out demons and many other biblical doctrines that are not on the list of "approved" Baptist beliefs. Many of them, like McKissic and me, were minding their own business when God invaded their ordered world with the Holy Spirit's untamed passion.

I believe it is well past time for all Bible-honoring evangelicals to loosen their restrictions and drop their fears of glossolalia. It was normative in New Testament times. It should be normative in the Church today. All of Jesus' disciples spoke in tongues. Everyone who was in the Upper Room on the Day of Pentecost spoke in tongues—including Jesus' mother. Paul prayed incessantly in tongues and gave the early Church detailed guidelines on the practice.

Why, then, has this precious spiritual gift been so maligned and ignored? Many fundamentalists, who claim to believe the Bible as literal, might as well take a pair of scissors and clip out whole portions of the New Testament, since they dismiss tongues as a valid gift. Many teach that the gift "passed away" with the early apostles—even though preaching, conversion, water baptism and every other New Testament grace continued without interruption.

There is a simple reason why tongues has been dismissed. The devil knows it is a powerful spiritual weapon, and he wants to steal it from our arsenal. We must recover it.

Why We Need Spiritual Language

In the first century, the apostle Paul taught that Christian faith could not be built on human intellect or reasoning. Greeks elevated the mind, but Paul cut through their vain philosophies, announcing that God's ways were higher than man's ways. He wrote the Corinthians:

> Yet we do speak wisdom among those who are mature; a wisdom, however, not of this age, nor of the rulers of this age, who are passing away; but we speak God's wisdom in a mystery, the hidden wisdom which God predestined before the ages to our glory.
>
> 1 Corinthians 2:6–7

Throughout his epistles Paul challenged the early Church to walk in the realm of the Spirit, not according to the flesh. He called the church to walk by faith and not by sight. And when he preached, he did it not with "persuasive words of wisdom" but in "demonstration of the Spirit and of power" (1 Corinthians 2:4). Paul also taught that the mind is actually at war with spiritual truth. He wrote: "But a natural man does not accept the things of the Spirit of God, for they are foolishness to him" (2:14).

Paul was a very intellectual man. He was a Pharisee of Pharisees. He had been trained by the most learned scholars of rabbinical Judaism. He knew the letter of the Law. He had superb oratorical skills. He also understood Greek philosophy and the intricacies of ancient languages. But when he came to Christ, he humbled himself and became, in essence, a babbling idiot. He received a miraculous gift of tongues that he did not understand. And yet he came to discover that this gift gave him a supernatural grace to commune with God on a deep level and to understand spiritual revelation.

Paul told the Corinthians that speaking in tongues, unless it is interpreted, has little value in a public meeting (1 Corinthians 14:6–15). He acknowledges that glossolalia has personal benefit to the believer when used privately, but he urges the Corinthians not to make a public spectacle out of this gift.

Paul says something curious in 1 Corinthians 14:2: "One who speaks in a tongue does not speak to men but to God; for no one understands, but in his spirit he speaks mysteries." How does this work? What goes on in the human brain when we speak in this form of prayer?

Amazingly, a team of researchers at the University of Pennsylvania discovered a key to this mystery in 2006. Researcher Andrew B. Newberg, author of *Why We Believe What We Believe*, and his colleagues used what is called neuroimaging to track blood flow to the brain. He used a test group of five Pentecostal women from the same Pentecostal church, measuring their brain waves when they sang a gospel song and when they spoke in tongues. He compared this with the brain waves of Buddhist monks and Catholic nuns in prayer. *USA Today* reported the findings:

> [Newberg's] scans found that when the subjects spoke, the frontal lobe showed less blood flow and lower activity than it did during the singing.
>
> Newberg previously examined Buddhist monks in meditation and Catholic nuns in prayer. Their brain scans showed that the frontal lobe lit up with more activity—the exact opposite of the tongue-speakers.
>
> "Our findings are very consistent with what people say they are feeling," Newberg says. "That they are not in charge of what is happening and are experiencing an intense sense of themselves in relation to God."[6]

Based on these findings, we see scientific evidence that something unusual happens in the human brain when we pray in tongues. This should not surprise us. God is employing a supernatural means to "override" our intellect. In order to do His miraculous work through us, He must, in essence, move our minds out of the way so that His higher truth and revelation can flow through us.

This would go a long way in explaining why all the disciples in the New Testament experienced speaking in tongues as an initial evidence of the baptism of the Holy Spirit. It happened to the believers at Pentecost; it happened to the Italian converts in Cornelius's house; it happened to the Gentiles in Ephesus and Corinth. Speaking in tongues seems to be some type of gateway into the spiritual experience.

This does not make speaking in tongues a more important gift. If anything, it can be viewed as a prerequisite baby step into the deeper things of God. But it does require the seeker to humble himself, lay aside intellectual pride and become like a child. Speaking in tongues makes no sense—either to the one who prays or to any person who might overhear him. Yet the Bible says when we pray in the Spirit we are speaking mysteries to God and edifying our spirit man. It is heaven's baffling way of bypassing our minds and imparting divine life and strength into our spirits.

Any Christian can speak in tongues. The gift is available to all (although the gift of public tongues, with interpretation, is treated differently by Paul in his letter to the Corinthians). But for us to receive this gift, we may have to wrestle with God as Jacob did at Peniel (Genesis 32:2–32). In that conflict, God dislocated the patriarch's hip and permanently wounded him so that he walked with a limp for the rest of his life.

So it is with the baptism of the Holy Spirit and the grace of spiritual language. When God gives us this gift He prevails over the strongest impulses of intellectual pride and human reasoning. Our natural inclination is to be in control, to have everything figured out and to base our lives on what we can see and taste and feel.

But God says no—we must trust Him. If we are going to live a fruitful life in the Spirit, we must let Him conquer our reasoning powers. We must let God strike our minds and wound us so that we can become as little children who believe without needing proof. We must humble ourselves, and be willing to speak heaven's mysteries without the privilege of understanding what we are saying.

Healing the Rift over Speaking in Tongues

My main reason for seeking the baptism in the Holy Spirit as a teenager was not so that I could speak in tongues, prophesy or attain the gift of healing. I just wanted more of God. I also wanted the boldness that the early disciples possessed, and I knew that boldness was a primary consequence of the infilling of the Spirit.

I also read in Scripture that the reason for the initial out-pouring of the Holy Spirit on the Day of Pentecost was to grant *dunamis*, or power, to the early Church. This is why I sought what I viewed as a second blessing of the Spirit: I wanted my life to affect those around me for Jesus Christ, and I knew I could not do that in my own feeble ability.

I did fully expect to experience the gifts of the Spirit after I prayed for an infilling. Yet when I did not receive the gift of tongues at the moment I prayed, I was not disappointed. I had not viewed the gifts as the goal of Spirit baptism—and I knew that I had been baptized in the Spirit. Still, I understood from reading the New Testament that the gift of tongues was available to all believers. So I remained open to receiving the gift. I continued to press in. Then, during my personal devotional time a day after asking for the baptism in the Spirit, I received the gift of tongues.

Traditional Pentecostal and charismatic theology says that tongues is the "initial evidence" of Holy Spirit baptism. Many pastors in the Assemblies of God, the Church of God (Cleveland, Tennessee), the Pentecostal Holiness denomination and various charismatic groups purport that a person is not truly filled with the Holy Spirit until he or she has spoken in tongues. Some traditional Pentecostal groups used to teach that seekers of the Spirit's blessing needed to "tarry" for long hours at church altars waiting for the promised gift. Many people would wait for months or even years for the evidence that they had been filled with the Spirit. They put all the emphasis on receiving tongues.

Some Pentecostals today are softening this stance, partly because large percentages of their own congregations do not speak in tongues. A study of fast-growing denominations in the 1990s showed that only 25 percent of the members of some Pentecostal churches claim to have received that spiritual gift.

Jack Hayford, a veteran Pentecostal pastor and the most prominent voice in the International Church of the Foursquare Gospel, opened up a new debate on this issue in his own denomination. While he still strongly advocates the gift of tongues as available to all believers, he began to call for balance on the issue.

In 1993 he told *Charisma* that he does not demand tongues as proof of the baptism in the Spirit, but views glossolalia as "a divine and desirable provision to assist every believer in prayer and praise." He added, "I accept the testimony of people in differing traditions who claim they are baptized in the Holy Spirit, whether they've spoken in tongues or not. Still, as I minister within my own tradition, I urge people to expect to speak with tongues when they receive the baptism with the Holy Spirit."[7]

The "initial evidence" teaching has created tensions in the Church. It has separated the "haves" from the "have nots." Many Pentecostals consider their non-Pentecostal brethren spiritually inferior, while some non-Pentecostals have adopted the dispensational view that speaking in tongues is a gift intended only for the early Church. Thus they believe that Pentecostals, by encouraging the practice of tongues-speaking, are promoting doctrinal error.

Is it possible that this colossal separation can be reconciled? I believe it can, but it will require loving acceptance and understanding on both sides.

Many of the popular charismatic Bible teachers of the 1970s, such as Dennis and Rita Bennett, Don Basham and Frances Hunter, furthered the doctrine of initial evidence. Most of those baptized with the Holy Spirit during the heyday of the charismatic renewal adopted the view that speaking in tongues is an essential ingredient in the Spirit-filled life. Many of the best-selling charismatic books of that period even offered practical steps to receiving a personal prayer language.

But in their popular book *The Holy Spirit and You*, the Bennetts offered an exhortation that deserves repeating:

> When a person receives the baptism with the Holy Spirit, it doesn't mean he's "arrived" spiritually. . . . Don't ever yield to the enemy's temptation to cause you to feel superior; pray for the fruit of humility; it is a good antidote. The baptism with the Holy Spirit is just the beginning of a new dimension in your Christian life, and it is still up to you whether you will grow or regress.[8]

I wish the Bennetts' words had been taken more to heart. Too many of us charismatics became puffed up with spiritual pride after our initial encounter with the Baptizer. We elevated our own views and looked down on those who disagreed with our interpretation of Scripture. Once I heard a prominent charismatic leader criticize the teachings of family counselor James Dobson because he wasn't "Spirit-filled." In this person's estimation, even evangelist Billy Graham was spiritually deficient—simply because he did not claim to speak in tongues.

Let's remember what Paul told the Corinthians when they were having a serious doctrinal dispute over the proper use of spiritual gifts:

> If the whole body were an eye, where would the sense of hearing be? If the whole body were an ear, where would the sense of smell be? But in fact God has arranged the parts in the body, every one of them, just as he wanted them to be. If they were all one part, where would the body be? As it is, there are many parts, but one body.
>
> The eye cannot say to the hand, "I don't need you!" And the head cannot say to the feet, "I don't need you!"
>
> 1 Corinthians 12:17–21, NIV

Paul clearly believed that all followers of Christ could exercise the gift of tongues. But in no way does he imply that those who speak in tongues are spiritually superior to those who do not. And nowhere does he endorse the idea that only those who speak in tongues fall into a special "Spirit-filled" category.

It is time we charismatics and Pentecostals shake ourselves loose from spiritual pride and claim the rest of the Body of Christ as equal members. If we simply accept the fact, as stated by Paul, that not all speak in tongues, then we can accept our Christian brothers and sisters as gifted in other, equally valid ways.

Non-Pentecostals likewise need to accept those who speak in tongues or exercise other spiritual gifts. Fundamentalist and evangelical leaders who believe that the miraculous power of the Holy Spirit was operative only during the dispensation of the early Church must not dismiss charismatics as ignorant and theologically misguided, an aberrant fringe group that has broken away from orthodoxy.

Perhaps as charismatic and Pentecostal churches continue to multiply, and as we rethink our dogmatism and doctrinal flaws, our fundamentalist brothers and sisters will reconsider the notion that the *charismata* have no place in today's Church, and more of our evangelical brothers and sisters will acknowledge that the Holy Spirit is indeed at work in our midst. Perhaps they will concede that we, too, have a legitimate role to play in the Body of Christ, and with our spiritual gifts and anointings complementing theirs. Perhaps they also will consider Paul's admonition in 1 Corinthians 14:39, "Do not forbid speaking in tongues" (NIV). Perhaps one day both groups can say to one another, "We have need of you."

How Deep Will You Go with God?

I often meet Christians who seem perfectly satisfied with where they are in their spiritual walks and some tell me they have no interest in receiving the baptism of the Holy Spirit. Others have prayed for this experience, but they do not want the gift of tongues. Sometimes they say to me: "Do I have to do that?"

The answer, of course, is no. You do not have to do it. But I have always had the attitude that I want everything God has for me. Why would I not want every one of His blessings? Sometimes this comes down to an issue of spiritual hunger. How desperate are you for God?

Every summer when I was a boy my parents took my sister and me to a family reunion in Alabama. My favorite part of the annual pilgrimage was the spring-fed public swimming pool where I spent countless hours with my cousin Chris. The best place to be on those hot, humid days in August was in that ice-cold water.

There was a problem with that pool, however. It was the temperature. The water was so cold that it took me several minutes to get my scrawny body all the way in. I can remember slowly easing into the shallow end, cringing and grimacing as I grasped the handrail by the steps.

It would have been easier to dispense with the torture and just dive headfirst into the deep end (or to be thrown in by an older cousin—which happened a few times against my will). But because the water was cold enough to turn my arms blue, I preferred to take ten minutes to slide into the pool inch by painful inch. And if anyone tried to splash me, I would run in terror and hide near the snack bar.

I think of those memories when I read about Ezekiel's vision of the river of God (Ezekiel 47:1–12). The prophet describes the river flowing out of the Temple in stages—first as a trickle, then as an ankle-deep stream, then knee-deep, then waist-deep and, finally, as a river that couldn't be crossed.

That river represents many things, including the promise that the Holy Spirit's influence in the world will grow deeper and stronger throughout history until the whole earth is covered with God's glory. But in a personal sense Ezekiel's vision is an invitation to go deeper. It beckons us to leave the shallowness of superficial spirituality.

Think about your own relationship with Jesus. What stage of His river are you swimming in?

The ankle-deep stage reminds me of the plastic kiddie pool I bought for my daughters when they were toddlers. The water was great to splash in, and it was safe for children who don't swim yet. But it was certainly not a place for grownups, as I learned when I jumped in the pool with my girls and sloshed most of the water into the yard.

The knee-deep water could be compared to a spiritual Jacuzzi. It's a place of refreshing but can easily lead to pampering and self-gratification. It's also confining; you'll never fit too many people in your personal spa. Many times we enjoy God's blessings and benefits, but we keep our faith contained in a shallow, us-four-and-no-more religious environment. It is what I call hot tub religion. It's all about us.

The waist-deep water is a critical stage. When I inched my way into that freezing pool in Alabama, I was always tempted to get out of the water when it hit my waist. We often want to stop when we reach halfway. When you get to the waist-deep water, you realize you must put your head under. You know it's either now or never.

Many of us get stuck at this point. God calls us to total surrender, but when we reach the halfway point we either turn back or park ourselves in perpetual limbo. We are either paralyzed by the fear of losing control or we stubbornly refuse to jettison the things that will sink us.

Finally we come to the depths of the river. The best thing we can do is dive in at this stage, where our head goes under and even our appearance is changed. It's true that in the deep end we cannot feel the bottom. There is no handrail to grasp. We must let go and allow His swift current to take us where He wants us.

As long as we can feel the bottom we are in control. When we let go, He steers our lives and takes us where He wants us to go. It is actually the best place to be, but no one is going to throw us into His river against our will.

If you have never taken the plunge into the river of the Spirit, now is your chance. You may have to swallow some fears. You may have to lay aside old religious mindsets or prejudices. But I can promise you that if you are filled with the Holy Spirit, and if you open your mouth to receive this language of heaven, you will not be disappointed.

The apostle Paul knew a power in prayer that few of us have discovered. He allowed the Spirit of God to pray through him, "with groanings too deep for words" (Romans 8:26). He learned how to use prayer as a weapon that could destroy demonic fortresses. He "labored" in prayer as a woman in childbirth. This was no ordinary praying—it was what the early disciples called "praying in the Holy Spirit" (Jude 20).

There is a realm of powerful prayer available to us that many of us have yet to experience. There is a prayer that moves mountains, deposes kings, breaks chains, woos back prodigals, opens the hearts of unbelievers, releases miracles and shakes nations. But we will never learn this kind of prayer in a book or master it by our mental ability. It is a purely spiritual art, and it must be taught by the Spirit. Open your heart to the Spirit's work and allow Him to use you as His vessel.

Questions for Discussion

1. Why do you think God gave the Church the gift of glossolalia, or speaking in tongues?
2. If this has been a part of your Christian experience, explain how it has helped you in your walk with God. If you have never spoken in tongues, share how you feel about the gift. Does it make you uncomfortable, or would you like to experience it?
3. Explain how a person who receives this gift could open themselves up to spiritual pride. How can this be avoided?
4. The prophet's vision of the river of God in Ezekiel 47:1-12 gives a picture of a river in four stages: (1) ankle-deep, (2) knee-deep, (3) waist-deep and (4) flood stage. Think about your own spiritual life and describe what level you feel you are in. What prevents you from going deeper?

If I have the gift of prophecy, and know all mysteries and all knowledge; and if I have all faith, so as to remove mountains, but do not have love, I am nothing.

1 Corinthians 13:2

Now I exhort you, brethren, by the name of our Lord Jesus Christ, that you all agree and that there be no divisions among you, but that you be made complete in the same mind and in the same judgment.

1 Corinthians 1:10

The Pentecostal power, when you sum it all up, is just more of God's love. If it does not bring more love, it is simply a counterfeit.

William J. Seymour, founder of the Azusa Mission and considered the father of the modern Pentecostal movement[1]

11

The Fire of Genuine Love

During a trip to India, I was asked to speak in several large churches in the southern state of Andra Pradesh. Just before my American team and I arrived for the first meeting—where two thousand Christians welcomed us by throwing flower petals—my host made an odd request.

"Please leave enough time at the end of the meeting for the ministry team to lay hands on every person," the pastor said.

Lay hands on two thousand people? I was willing to oblige, but I wondered how it would be possible, since I had only five people helping me. Plus, I had been warned that six thousand people would attend another church service we were scheduled to visit that afternoon. And after that, there would be a 5 p.m. service in yet another large church. How could we possibly take this much time to do hands-on altar ministry?

I soon learned why laying on of hands is so essential in India. The people we were ministering to were Dalits, otherwise known as "untouchables." Hindu tradition tells these poorest of India's poor that they are unworthy of any human respect. They are considered subhuman, doomed to suffer lifelong poverty and disease. They are ignored by Hinduism's gods and hated by people in higher castes. It has been this way for centuries.

Some 340 million Dalits live in India today, more than one-fourth of the huge nation's population. They are starting to question whether Hinduism has anything to offer them, especially after they hear stories of how Jesus Christ ate with outcasts, conversed with Samaritans and healed untouchable lepers.

In that first morning service I agreed to minister to the people in the following way. Everyone in the church lined up, and my team members and I laid hands on each one. I immediately could tell something supernatural was happening. The love of God was pouring out of us. The people were weeping, and this caused me to cry, too.

As I placed my hands on the heads and shoulders of these precious people, it angered me that the Hindu religion had convinced them God did not care about them. Yet I could rejoice that day knowing that Satan's lies had been exposed and defeated. What an awesome Savior we have—one who was willing to condescend to this sinful world and love us. We were all untouchables, but He cleansed us!

Each time I preached during that two-week trip in April, I made sure we laid hands on everyone after each meeting. I embraced some of them, knowing that Christian affection—empowered by the Holy Spirit—has the power to break the diabolical curse that has kept the Dalits in a spiritual prison for centuries.

God's love has an uncanny way of crossing immovable boundaries. That is why thousands of Dalits are coming to Christ today. Every Dalit conversion is chipping away at India's oppressive caste structure. "The Dalit Christian revival is a phenomenon that no man has strategized or planned," says Sam Paul, a respected Indian church leader from Hyderabad. "It was orchestrated in God's heart."

"It is God's doing—a miracle," adds Raja J. Solomon, who works with the Operation Mobilization ministry in the northern city of Lucknow. He says that an overwhelming response to the Gospel among Dalits, especially in northern regions, began in 2001 and "cannot be explained."

During my visit I met numerous Dalit pastors who have seen unprecedented responses to the Gospel since the late 1990s. So many Dalits are embracing Christianity that India is facing a political crisis. Dalit Christians who have been denied equal rights for decades now are demanding that the government stop religious discrimination, which has prevented Dalits from getting jobs, owning property and enjoying equal educational opportunities.

This social shift has major implications. When the caste system crumbles, it will be as significant as the end of South African apartheid or the fall of Soviet Communism. I believe that in our lifetime, as the Holy Spirit's work continues in India, we will witness the complete unraveling of this diabolical social structure.

God's Love Destroys Racism

I was raised in Alabama and Georgia, where racist attitudes were acceptable even in the church. When I was just a boy, some of the deacons in our church in Montgomery tried to pressure my father to stand outside the sanctuary with a baseball bat to discourage African Americans from visiting. Thankfully, my dad refused.

Later, a relative sat me down and gave me what she considered to be an important lesson: "Lee, the black people have their church, and the white people have their church, and that's the way the Lord wants it."

But I somehow knew this advice wasn't sound. It seemed contradictory to the essence of the Gospel. Jesus went out of His way to break social barriers. He even went to Samaria—a place no other kosher rabbi would dare visit. (Samaritans were considered unclean because of their racial makeup.) After Jesus ministered to the divorced woman at the well, He stayed there two days—eating Samaritan food, living in a Samaritan house and soaking in Samaritan culture (John 4:40).

Later, when he was about to ascend into heaven, Jesus listed Samaria as one of the primary assignments of His followers. He told them: "But you will receive power when the Holy Spirit has come upon you; and you shall be My witnesses both in Jerusalem, and in all Judea *and Samaria*, and even to the remotest part of the earth" (Acts 1:8, emphasis added).

We tend to forget that Jesus' first disciples were all Jews who were raised by kosher Jewish mothers. They did not feel comfortable in Gentile environments, and they were very uncomfortable when Jesus led them into Samaria the first time. Now, after His resurrection, He commissioned them to go there again!

In Acts 10, God calls the apostle Peter to go to the house of an Italian man, Cornelius. This was unheard of in those days. Jews did not visit Gentile houses. I am sure Peter felt awkward when he walked into that home and smelled the Italian food, which probably consisted of meats he would never touch. Yet the Bible says that when he preached to those Italians, they were filled with the Holy Spirit.

The Gospel always compels us to cross ethnic and racial boundaries. It requires us to die to any prejudice or racism. We cannot truly walk in the power of the Spirit if we have such attitudes. It is not enough to love people you feel comfortable with. Genuine love goes the extra mile. It is extended to people who are not like us.

Ever since I have been filled with the Holy Spirit I've felt a strong push from the Lord to venture outside my cultural comfort zone. I have befriended immigrants from Brazil, Russia, India and the Middle East. I have preached in black, white and Hispanic churches. I have eaten all kinds of foreign foods—including some meats I couldn't identify in China.

And when I go to foreign countries, I end up ministering to people on the fringes of society.

God's love will always push you to the edge. One Saturday morning, as I waited for my daughter's car to be repaired, I decided to get a haircut. Across the street a sign read "HAIR," and I figured I would try a new place for a change—even though I was unfamiliar with the neighborhood. When I walked into the place, I realized it was a shop catering to African Americans.

Everyone in the place was black, and they all gave me slightly puzzled stares when I came through the door. They probably weren't used to seeing middle-aged white men in the place for haircuts. I immediately smelled chemicals I'd never smelled before. About eight women were seated in chairs on the left side of the salon, and I learned that many of them had been there for two hours getting relaxer treatments or elaborate weaves. Several men were in the cramped lobby waiting in line for the one male stylist who specialized in men's hair.

I had an awkward choice to make. I could turn and walk out, and risk sending the message that I didn't want to be in a black hair salon. Or I could do what Jesus would do. I quickly decided that He had led me to this place.

I gave my name to the receptionist—a kind-faced, middle-aged woman who was carrying on a spirited conversation about her unexpected pregnancy with one of the female customers. I was told that "Devon" would be cutting my hair when he finished with the four men in front of me.

I could feel the stares more intensely as I thumbed through copies of *Ebony* and *Black Enterprise*. The receptionist looked at me every minute or so with a nervous smile. I asked her about her large family and told her about my four teenage girls. We suddenly had a lot in common.

While a wall-mounted television blared a rerun of *The Proud Family*, the whirring of hair clippers blended with a dozen conversations to make the room buzz. There was

203

a sense of community in this place that I'd never felt in the suburban salon I visit once a month. These people knew one another, shared their family news and even swapped prayer requests.

I was starting to feel quite at home, but lots of questions were going through my mind. Do some of these folks want me to leave? Will they laugh when I walk out of here? Does Devon know how to cut a white guy's hair? All the men in front of me were getting their heads shaved except for one, who was having his short hair platted in tiny patches and adorned with beads. I did not want beads, a shaved cut or a "low, low fade," which is shorter than a buzz cut.

When I climbed into Devon's chair I immediately pushed past the awkwardness. "So is there really any difference when it comes to cutting black or white hair?" I asked.

Devon laughed. "No, man. It's all just hair." He laughed again when I admitted that I had used Afro Sheen on my curls when I was a teenager.

Devon did a great job on my hair. Then I told the receptionist I hoped she would have no complications with her pregnancy. A lot of eyes followed me as I walked to the door. Some of them looked dumbfounded, as if I had broken an unwritten social rule.

I just smiled and waved. It felt good to break some stereotypes—and make new friends in the process.

Pentecost Will Not Be Confined

Satan has used lies and racial stereotypes to divide and isolate us. But when we spend time with one another, we discover how flimsy the devil's barriers really are. I hope you will venture outside your own safety zone and start crashing through the cultural blockades that separate people in your community.

We still have a long way to go when it comes to racial healing. Some old wounds are still bleeding. Many churches are still politely segregated. Walls of suspicion and mistrust still divide people of faith. We are afraid of getting our hands "dirty" by crossing these barriers.

The Pharisees had a strict religious code of hygiene, and they stayed aloof from all non-Jews. Yet when they criticized Jesus because He did not require His disciples to follow these codes, He called them hypocrites. Then He immediately went to the region of Tyre—outside the borders of Israel—and ministered to a desperate Gentile woman who was considered unclean by the Jews (Mark 7:24–30).

Jesus was clearly showing the Pharisees that true faith has nothing to do with living in a sanitized, racially segregated world. Jesus popped their bubble by venturing into Gentile territory, setting up His base in a Gentile house (7:24) and casting a demon out of a Gentile woman's daughter.

Jesus told the Pharisees—and showed them—that their holier-than-thou traditions actually nullified the Word of God. They were obsessed with washing their hands and dishes to keep themselves pure; Jesus was focused on touching the untouchables of society so that God's love and mercy could spread to everyone. We today have a choice: sterile religion or radical compassion.

I'm convinced we won't achieve true racial reconciliation until we all become more intentional about it. Healing won't happen if we don't make it a priority. What will it require? If we truly want to be a prophetic people, the Church must address racism from every angle:

- We must challenge Christians to let go of racial offenses rather than tolerating a climate of bitterness and resentment.
- We must build multiethnic churches led by multiethnic leadership teams.
- We must be willing to feel the pain of those who have suffered discrimination so we can truly "bear one another's burdens" (Galatians 6:2). That means we have

to educate ourselves about the history of racism in our own communities—and dialog with the people who have been most affected. It means we have to ask—and be willing to listen.

Don't Run from Your Nineveh!

In the eighth century B.C., Jonah participated in one of the most unusual prayer meetings in history. It happened at the bottom of the sea inside a giant fish. With damp seaweed wrapped around his head and his skin bleached by digestive juices, the renegade prophet sat on the fish's slimy stomach membrane and gasped for breath amidst the foul odor of eels, crabs and barnacles.

In total darkness Jonah prayed from the salty depths: "Those who regard vain idols forsake their faithfulness, but I will sacrifice to You with the voice of thanksgiving. That which I have vowed I will pay. Salvation is from the LORD" (Jonah 2:8–9).

Sometimes we must sink to the lowest point before we turn to God. That's what Jonah did. From what could have been a watery grave, he got a second chance to obey.

The giant fish swam hundreds of miles eastward, back toward the Phoenician shore, and vomited the repentant prophet onto dry land. Then the word of the Lord came to Jonah a second time: "Arise, go to Nineveh the great city" (3:2). It had not been an easy process, but Jonah now understood his priorities: He knew God was serious about crossing cultural barriers.

You see, Nineveh was a city that no Jew cared to visit. So when Jonah finally arrived there and heralded his message, it caused a citywide commotion. Within hours, everyone was talking about the Jewish prophet who spoke of divine judgment. All the inhabitants of the Assyrian capital, including the king, put on sackcloth and called on the name of the God of Israel because of Jonah's dire warning.

206

God touched an entire city with His amazing forgiveness because one reluctant man finally repented of his racism and fulfilled his divine assignment to warn a despised and alien people.

All of us can relate to this story. We are called to minister to the faithless Ninevehs of our generation—our workplaces, campuses, neighborhoods, cities and beyond. Each of us is called to be a missionary with a specific assignment. But often we run in the opposite direction of our assignment because of fear of failure, insecurity about our weaknesses, disappointment about a past ministry experience or just plain selfishness.

Jonah hired a boat to take him to Tarshish, which was about as far as you could go from Nineveh in those days. (Bible scholars say it was in eastern Spain, possibly a mining outpost near Gibraltar.) Perhaps he was going there to strike it rich. But he never reached his Mediterranean hideaway. God found him asleep in the hold of the boat and sent a storm to rouse him. Within a few hours, Jonah was thrown overboard and ended up as fish food.

Do you find yourself in Jonah's story? Are you running from God's call on your life? Have you tried to drown out the cries of lost people? Have you hired a luxury ship to take you to a comfort zone where you don't have to think about the needs of your Nineveh? Has God called you simply to love people you don't like to be around?

Many of us are in Jonah's boat. We don't like to hear sermons about evangelism. We're not interested in the crucified life. We've shunned sacrifice. We don't want to admit our racism. Instead of making the Great Commission our priority, we've fallen asleep with our iPods playing perky messages about success and prosperity. But God has sent a storm to rouse a distracted, disobedient Church out of its slumber. We must take the same steps Jonah did.

First, we must *wake up*. Jonah's disobedience put the sailors on his ship in peril. Did you realize that when we shirk our responsibility to share the Gospel of Christ, others perish? We must get out of our beds of spiritual lethargy and stop ignoring the cries of the unbelieving.

Jonah's real problem was that he lacked love. He didn't want to go to Nineveh because he looked down on those people. He had a smug form of religious racism. He felt superior, and his pride prevented him from feeling God's compassion for them. Another reason he ran from God's assignment was because he knew the Lord would forgive the people if they repented—and Jonah didn't want that. He didn't care.

We often respond the same way. Oftentimes we are more interested in getting personal prophecies, having heavenly visitations or interpreting our dreams. We've become ingrown and self-absorbed. But an alarm has sounded!

Second, we must *look up*. Sometimes God allows difficult circumstances to bring His Church to repentance. Could this be one reason our economy is squeezing us to a breaking point? Has God sent a storm to blow away the materialism that has made us fat, comfortable and proud? Jonah was stripped to the bare essentials by the time he landed in the fish's belly. It was a scary process, yet a loving God watched over him. The fact is that many of us will face some darkness and discomfort before we emerge empowered for a coming season of revival.

Third, we must *embrace our call*. When Jonah repented, he declared: "Salvation is from the LORD" (2:9). How desperately the American church today must embrace again the message of salvation. We must stop running. We must yield to God's love. The Lord wants to use all of us to reach people for Him. He has given all of us the message of reconciliation, and we must reclaim it, preach it and live it anew.

The Bible tells us that Jonah was fleeing the presence of the Lord (Jonah 1:3). This shows us that God's *presence* cannot be separated from His *mission*. If we want His presence, we must be involved in His work. It is not enough to sing worship songs all day; God has a burden on His heart. *For God so loved the world!* If we refuse to allow His Holy Spirit to use us to reach the lost, then we are rejecting His presence.

Jonah tried to flee as far as possible from Nineveh, but the God of second chances used a strange vessel to get the prophet back on course. Jonah spent three days in the darkness of the fish's stomach, stewing in digestive juices. When the fish vomited him on land, he was better prepared to speak heaven's words.

Paul tells us that the Lord cannot accomplish His mission without those who will speak for Him. He writes: "How will they believe in Him whom they have not heard? And how will they hear without a preacher?" (Romans 10:14).

The Christian life is not about me and my needs—it is a call to deny myself and share the forgiveness of Jesus with everyone around me. I urge you, if you are a fugitive from the call of God, please turn yourself in today. You can ask Him for a fresh infilling of the Holy Spirit—and you can expect that He will baptize you afresh with His genuine love so you can minister to those around you.

Questions for Discussion

1. Pentecost broke down the racial barriers between people. How should this impact your daily life?
2. Can you think of people you contact regularly who are "untouchables"? How can you reach them?
3. Why is racism contradictory to the love of God?
4. When you meditate on the story of Jonah, how do you relate to him? What is your "Nineveh"? Can you think of any way in which you are running from your divine assignment?

And behold, I am sending forth the promise of My Father upon you; but you are to stay in the city until you are clothed with power from on high.

Luke 24:49

Trying to do the Lord's work in your own strength is the most confusing, exhausting, and tedious of all work. But when you are filled with the Holy Spirit, then the ministry of Jesus just flows out of you.

Corrie ten Boom, Dutch author (1892–1985)[1]

Let us bow very low before God, in waiting for His grace to fill and to sanctify us. We do not want a power which God might allow us to use, while our inner part is unsanctified. . . . We should seek, therefore, not only a baptism of power, but a baptism of holiness; we should seek that the inner nature be sanctified by the indwelling of Jesus, and then other power will come as needed.

Andrew Murray[2]

12

How to Have Your Own Personal Pentecost

One of my life goals is to stay hot for God. When I look at the spiritual giants of the Bible, I see men and women who carried a holy fire inside them—a fire that produced much more than personal piety. After heaven's coals touched their lips, the flames drove them to pursue God's radical agenda.

The prophets of the Old Testament knew this fire. Jeremiah felt as if God's flames were shut up in his bones (Jeremiah 20:9), and his spiritual passion drove him to weep in the streets as he confronted the sins of Israel. Elijah called down God's fire from heaven and relentlessly opposed Jezebel's plot against God's faithful remnant. Huldah's fiery prophetic zeal provoked King Josiah to destroy all the idols in the Temple. King David said the zeal of the Lord "consumed" him (Psalm 69:9)—and Jesus cited that verse when He drove the money-changers out of the Temple with a whip.

This fire blazed in the hearts of believers who were torn apart by Caesar's lions in the first century. It burned in the hearts of the Reformers who risked their lives to publish the

Bible. If more recent spiritual heroes such as Charles Finney, George Whitefield, John Wesley and Catherine Booth had anything in common, it was their white-hot zeal. Lukewarm Christians never changed their world.

You may think that such unusual fervor is an emotion reserved only for full-time evangelists or missionaries. But the apostle Paul tells us that *all Christians* should have a spiritual temperature that reaches the boiling point. In Romans 12:11 he commands us to be "fervent in spirit." The Greek word for fervent is *zeo*, which means "to boil like hot liquid or to glow like hot metal."

I see this boiling hot zeal in Christian heroes of the past two centuries. These are my true heroes. When I read the writings of John Wesley, Charles Finney, Charles Spurgeon, Andrew Murray, William Seymour, E. M. Bounds, Watchman Nee, Oswald Chambers, A. B. Simpson, Brother Andrew or Corrie ten Boom, their words speak more deeply to me than most contemporary authors. For these people, the baptism of the Holy Spirit was not just a momentary experience or an emotional high. They walked through serious trials and suffering. Total surrender was their lifestyle.

As we seek God for a new season of spiritual renewal (and none of us at this point knows what the new movement will look like), I believe we need to look backward as we move forward. There is something from the past that we must recover. We can learn it from these fire-tested saints.

The charismatic renewal of the last forty years has been a time of refreshing for the Church, to be sure. But I fear it was short-lived because we allowed it to be shallow. And this is because we have trivialized the message of Pentecost. We cheapened it. We made it easy for anyone to come to a church altar, stand in a line and have hands laid on them. They could fall backward, speak in tongues and—bam!—they've been anointed by the Spirit.

Is it really that easy? I am not suggesting that we have to work for the anointing of the Spirit. The grace of God is free.

But a sanctified life is not something we receive in a line. It is something we wrestle for. If the early disciples tarried for weeks before the blessing of Pentecost, why do we encourage people to pray for this blessing before they've had a chance to even count the cost of discipleship?

During the holiness revivals of the late 1800s, America's preachers called God's people to embrace the baptism of the Holy Spirit. Their focus was not on speaking in tongues or the gifts of the Spirit; churches in those days did not understand that revelation from God's Word. But they proclaimed convincingly that God had a second blessing for His people. They saw the baptism of the Holy Spirit as an act of full consecration. They saw it as a step into the sanctified life. They cherished it as a pearl of great price.

This same understanding permeated the early Pentecostal revivals of the twentieth century. Preachers such as William Seymour, C. H. Mason and Gaston B. Cashwell did not view the baptism of the Holy Spirit simply as a momentary experience of empowerment. They saw it as an introduction into a life of holiness and consecration. They expected the baptism of the Holy Spirit to transform weak, hesitant, sinsick churchgoers into courageous, impassioned, holy, fire-breathing disciples.

Where do you stand today? You may have never asked God to baptize you in the Holy Spirit. Or perhaps you had this experience, but you recognize now that your fire has been left to smolder. Perhaps the flame burned brightly at one point, but you became distracted by life's challenges. Perhaps you had a moral failure. Or perhaps you dipped your foot into carnal pleasures and kept going back for more, lulled into spiritual apathy with the encouragement of a hell-bent culture. Or perhaps problems in your church or ministry soured your attitude and you became disillusioned.

Spiritual zeal must be rekindled regularly. It is your responsibility to fan the flames. Perhaps you would like to pray for a fresh baptism of the Holy Spirit. First, prepare your heart as you ponder the remainder of this chapter. Then I encourage you to use the prayer guide at the conclusion so that you can settle this matter with God.

What Is Your Spiritual Temperature?

Many Christians struggle to live a life of faith because they have not surrendered their hearts fully to the Lord. They live on the proverbial fence, constantly wavering. They find it hard to believe that God loves them. They stumble into habitual sin constantly. They struggle with the simplest of spiritual disciplines.

The reason they seem to lack the ability to follow Christ wholeheartedly is that they have not fully yielded to His grace. Yes, they said a prayer of confession and asked Jesus to come and live in their hearts. But they are not fully convinced that Jesus loves them and that He gave His life for them on the cross. And they have not fully entrusted their lives into His care.

Other Christians serve Jesus faithfully for years but then crawl off of His altar. It is possible for any of us to run from God, just as Jonah did. Even some of the greatest spiritual giants of the past went through difficult times of wandering, doubt or discouragement. Sometimes because life's challenges hit us hard, we begin to backslide. Even if you have thrown in the towel, it is not too late to get back onto His altar and ask for a new visitation of His Spirit.

Perhaps you believe that Christ is your Savior, but you have never truly yielded to Him as your Lord. He cannot be one and not the other. He is both Savior and Lord. He purchased your life when He redeemed you; now, He asks that you surrender your will, emotions, disappointments, failures, fears, plans, goals and dreams to Him. Making this important decision will certainly increase the spiritual temperature in your life.

Yielding to Jesus' Lordship is an act of faith as well as of consecration. Consecration is defined as: "The devoting or setting apart of anything to the worship or service of God." In the Old Testament, anything used in the Tabernacle or the Temple had to be consecrated first. The priests, the furniture, the utensils and the offerings were all consecrated. Most of all, God desired His people to be consecrated as *His*. The Lord told Israel: "You shall consecrate yourselves therefore and be holy, for I am the LORD your God" (Leviticus 20:7).

As you prepare yourself to be freshly baptized in the Holy Spirit, ask yourself these questions:

1. Have you broken all ties to your sinful past? Jesus commanded us not only to believe and repent but also to be baptized in water. In water baptism we demonstrate that we belong to Christ. We also are renouncing the devil and any idols we have served in the past. If you have been involved in a false religion, the occult or any form of idolatry, it is especially important to break their control through your obedience in baptism.

2. Are you ruthlessly dealing with all known sin in your life? Many Christians live in a continual state of lukewarmness because they are not willing to lay the axe to the root of their sin. God wants you to bring all your sinful habits into the burning light of His presence. That will require you to be brutally honest by confessing to a trusted Christian friend who can pray for you.

3. Are you grieved by the blatant sinfulness of the culture around you? Jesus never called us to isolate ourselves from unbelievers. But if we compromise with the world's values, we will grow cold. Our entertainment choices, close relationships or selfish pleasures can subtly lure us away from wholehearted devotion. If you have pitched your tent too close to Sodom, your friendship with darkness will snuff out your spiritual passion.

4. Are you pursuing the things of God with more passion than other personal interests? During the days of the prophet

Haggai, Israel was guilty of the sin of misplaced priorities. People were building their own houses while God's house lay in ruins (Haggai 1:2–5). You may have admirable goals that don't seem "wrong" in themselves, but your desire for a career, material success, recognition, a mate or a stress-free life may be what is sapping your zeal.

5. Are you intimate with God? Spiritual zeal is not about how long you pray, how many times you go to church each week or how many Bible verses you have memorized. True passion for God is fueled when you are close to Him. If your faith has become a rote formula, a dry tradition or an empty shell, run back into His arms and let Him melt your cold, backslidden heart.

You are called to be a worshiper, and intimacy with God requires devotion. Do the distractions of entertainment, work and relationships fill up your time? Does your heart beat fastest for Him, or have other interests replaced your first love? Do you truly live to please the Father alone, or have you become addicted to the praises of men?

6. Do you harbor unforgiveness? Do you have resentment toward anyone who has wronged you? If so, a bitter poison is taking its toll—and you could infect others and start an epidemic. You must forgive every offense, release every judgment and drop every grudge. Are you jealous of another brother because he makes more money or seems more successful? You must rejoice with him instead of secretly resenting his blessings.

7. Do you need an attitude adjustment? If you don't walk with the limp of humility, pride will cause you to strut. Do you radiate the love, joy and peace of the Holy Spirit—or are you better known for anxiety, rudeness, cutting remarks and irritability? What happens when you are under pressure? Do you manifest the sweet demeanor of a trusting heart, or throw a childish temper tantrum?

8. Does your tongue need an examination? Does grateful thanksgiving pour out of your mouth regularly, or do you spend most of your time griping and complaining? Are you blessing people regularly with encouragement, or tearing them down with criticism and negativity? Have you grown so callous that you don't feel convicted when you malign a person's character by talking about him behind his back?

9. **What's happening in your most private areas?** We can't view sexual purity as optional. You cannot be spiritually healthy if you don't hate sin. Does lust control any area of your life? Have you bowed your knee to the spirit of Baal, who controls our culture with pornography and perversion? Do you flee from sexual temptation the very second you are confronted with an image? Or do you toy with it as long as you know no one is looking?

10. **Do you have compassion for those who don't know Jesus?** If it has been a while since you've shared your faith with a non-Christian, that's a good indication that your zeal has waned. When the fire of God rages inside us, we cannot hold it in! And nothing will stoke your spiritual passion more than leading someone to Christ.

Dealing with an Unwilling Spirit

The Bible tells us that the Holy Spirit is sensitive. He can be grieved (Ephesians 4:30) and quenched (1 Thessalonians 5:19). This means we can do things that cause Him to withdraw His presence and blessing in our lives. To quench the Spirit is to throw cold water on His flames.

I believe we quench the Holy Spirit in many ways. One is with doubt and intellectual pride. If we base all our decisions on what we know, we leave no room for the realm of faith. The Spirit speaks to us in spiritual terms that cannot be understood by the natural man. As long as we live in that realm we will never be filled with the Spirit's power.

Another way we quench the Spirit is with religious tradition. Throughout history, religious people have persecuted believers

217

who were led by the Holy Spirit. Just as the Pharisees hated Jesus and wanted Him dead, Christians who say they love God will criticize and oppose genuine spiritual renewal.

We also quench the Spirit with fear. You will never fully embrace the Holy Spirit's work if you are afraid of the supernatural. We must get beyond this. If you read the book of Acts, you will see that God did many strange and unusual things in the early Church! He not only healed the sick and raised the dead, but He shook buildings, caused doors to open by themselves, struck false prophets blind, gave people visions and transported a man instantaneously from one city to another.

The Holy Spirit's work can seem strange to us. But we must not let fear stop us from embracing His work. We must be people of faith who expect God to do miracles.

We can also quench the Spirit through unconfessed sin. This is why it is so important for us to be in close relationship with other Christians in a faith community. God never intended for us to walk alone. We need close friends who can help bear our burdens, share our struggles, pray for us and listen to our confession when necessary. Living a transparent life gives victory over any sin.

One of the most common ways we quench the Holy Spirit is by harboring an unwilling spirit. I had a dramatic experience in 1999 in which the Lord helped me overcome this. My church in Florida sponsored a conference on the Holy Spirit. At the close of one service I was lying on the floor near the altar asking God for a touch of His power. Several other people were kneeling at the communion rail and praying quietly for each other as soft music played in the background.

Suddenly I began to have a vision. In my mind I could see a large pipeline, at least eight feet in diameter. I was looking at it from the inside, and I could see a shallow stream of golden liquid flowing at the bottom. The oil in the giant pipe was only a few inches deep.

I began a conversation with the Lord. "What are You showing me?" I asked.

"This is the flow of the Holy Spirit in your life," He answered.

It was not an encouraging picture; it was pitiful! The capacity of the pipeline was huge—enough to convey tons of oil. Yet only a trickle was evident.

Then I noticed something else: Several large valves lined the sides of the pipeline, and each of them was shut. I wanted to ask the Lord why there was so little oil in my life. Instead I asked: "What are those valves, and why are they closed?"

"Those represent the times when you said no. Why should I increase the level of anointing if you aren't available to use it?"

The words stung. I wondered—when had I said no to God? I was overcome with emotion and began to repent. I recalled different excuses I had made and limitations I had placed on how He could use me.

For example, I had told Him I didn't want to be in front of crowds because I wasn't a good speaker. I had told Him that if I couldn't preach like T. D. Jakes does, then I didn't want to speak at all. I had told Him I didn't want to address certain issues or go certain places. I also knew I had a fear of flying because I did not like turbulence on airplanes. I recognized that this fear had become a blockage in my life.

After a while I began to envision something else in my spirit. I pictured a huge crowd of African men, assembled as if they were in a large arena. I saw myself preaching to them.

Nobody had ever asked me to minister in Africa, but I knew at that moment I needed to surrender my will. All I could think to say was the prayer of Isaiah: "Here am I. Send me!" (Isaiah 6:8). I told God I would go anywhere and say anything He asked. I laid my insecurities, fears and inhibitions on the altar. I repented of my unwilling spirit.

You can probably guess what happened. Two years later, I stood behind a pulpit inside a sports arena in Port Harcourt,

Nigeria. As I addressed a crowd of eight thousand pastors who had assembled there for a training conference, I remembered seeing their faces in that vision. And I realized that God had opened a new valve in my life that day in 1999. Because I had said yes, He had increased the flow of His oil so that it could reach thousands.

Since that day I have traveled to more than 24 countries, preaching in churches, conferences and outdoor meetings. I had always considered myself a shy person and never dreamed I would be involved at such a level of public ministry. I saw myself as a journalist and preferred to hide behind my pen. But God had other plans. And He had to fill me with His Holy Spirit—and deal with all my excuses—to take me where He wanted me.

I encourage you to ask God for more. To do this, make sure you have surrendered every condition that you have ever placed on your obedience.

Those of us who call ourselves charismatics have a habit of asking for more of God's power and anointing. But what do we use it for? We love to go to the altar to get a touch from God. We love the goose bumps, the shaking, the emotion of the moment. We love to fall on the floor and receive prayer for more anointing. But I am afraid many of us are faking it. We get up off the floor and live just the way we want to.

If we truly want to be empowered, we must offer God an unqualified yes. We must crucify every no. We must leave our fears, insecurities and unwillingness at the cross.

Search your own heart today and see if there are any closed valves. Before you ask Him for a fresh baptism of the Spirit, make sure all is on the altar. As you surrender, the locked channels of your heart will open, and the flow of His oil will amaze you.

Receive His fresh anointing. I pray that the flame of the Spirit will become a raging fire shut up in your bones. I pray that, like Jeremiah, you will not be able to contain His zeal. And I pray that this fresh fire will fall from heaven, consume all the dross of our past mistakes and grant the Church a new grace to fulfill the Great Commission in our generation.

Questions for Discussion

1. If you were to take your spiritual temperature at this point in your life, what would it be? Would you be at the boiling point, or lukewarm, or cold—or somewhere in between?
2. Why is it important to consecrate ourselves before praying for an infilling of the Holy Spirit?
3. Read over the list of ten numbered questions in the middle of the chapter. Identify an area in which you know you need to surrender fully to God.
4. There are things listed that hinder the flow of the Holy Spirit: (1) doubt and intellectual pride, (2) religious tradition, (3) fear of the supernatural, (4) unconfessed sin and (5) an unyielded spirit. Which of these present the greatest problem for you?
5. Do you desire to pray for the infilling of the Holy Spirit, either for the first time or for a fresh anointing? If so, use the prayer guide that immediately follows.

How to Be Baptized in the Holy Spirit

When we encounter Christ and put our trust in Him, we are "born again" (John 3:3). At that point, we receive the Holy Spirit in our hearts. This is the most important decision we will ever make. This happened to the disciples of Jesus in John 20:22: "(Jesus) breathed on them and said to them, 'Receive the Holy Spirit.'"

But before Jesus ascended to heaven, He told His disciples to wait in Jerusalem until the "promise of [the] Father" had come (Luke 24:49). He told them that if they would wait there, they would be "clothed with power from on high." And in Acts 1:8, Jesus told His followers they would receive "power" to be His witnesses.

So the disciples waited in Jerusalem for many days, praying near the Temple. On the Day of Pentecost, which was fifty days after Jesus had died on the cross, something amazing happened. The Holy Spirit was poured out on the early Church. This is described in Acts 2:1–4. The Bible says that when the Spirit came, the disciples were filled (another word is "baptized") with the Spirit.

This shows us that there are two separate experiences we can have with God. One is salvation, in which we receive God's amazing forgiveness and a new nature. The Holy Spirit comes to live inside us, and He becomes our Teacher, our Comforter and our Helper.

The second experience is the baptism of the Holy Spirit, in which the Holy Spirit who is already in us flows forth. "Baptized in the Spirit" means "completely immersed in the Spirit." Jesus never wanted us to rely on our own ability to do the work of ministry. He wants to do it through us. So He fills us with the Holy Spirit to empower us with His ability.

When we have this experience, the Holy Spirit's power fills us so full that He flows forth. Also, when we are baptized in the Spirit, unusual "gifts of the Holy Spirit"—which are listed in 1 Corinthians 12:8–10—begin to be manifested in our lives. We experience His supernatural power. These gifts include prophecy, discernment, miracles, healing and speaking in unknown tongues.

When people were baptized in the Holy Spirit in the New Testament church, the Bible says they all spoke in tongues (Acts 2:1–4; 4:31; 10:44–48; 19:1–7). Many Christians get hung up on the matter of speaking in tongues because it seems strange. It's actually not strange at all. It is a very special form of prayer that any Christian can experience. When we pray in our heavenly prayer language, we are praising God and also strengthening ourselves spiritually. Speaking in tongues helps us become mighty in the Spirit. Being baptized in the Holy Spirit is not something we have to qualify for. Any Christian can ask, and Jesus is ready to do it. You can pray by yourself or you can ask someone else to pray for you.

Here are the simple steps you can take to be filled with the Holy Spirit:

1. **Prepare your heart.** The Holy Spirit is holy. He is compared to a fire (Matthew 3:11), which means he purifies sin and burns up that which is not Christlike in our

lives. Make sure you have confessed all known sin and made your heart ready for His infilling.

2. **Ask Jesus to baptize you in the Spirit.** You do not need to jump through hoops to get God's attention. He is eager to answer your request. Jesus is the One who baptizes us in the Spirit, so ask Him—and expect Him to answer.

3. **Receive the infilling.** Begin to thank Him for this miracle. The Holy Spirit's power is filling your life. If you feel your mind is clouded with doubts, just praise the Lord. Focus your mind on Him and not on yourself.

4. **Release your prayer language.** The moment you are filled with the Spirit, you will receive the ability to speak in your heavenly prayer language. You may feel the words bubbling up inside of you. You may begin to hear the words in your mind. Open your mouth and begin to speak, trusting the Lord to give you this new, supernatural language.

5. **Step out in boldness.** After you have been baptized in the Holy Spirit, one of the first things you will notice is a new boldness. The Holy Spirit does not like to hide. He wants you to speak about Jesus to those around you—and He will give you surprising courage. Now, expect Him to use you in surprising ways.

Notes

Preface

1. Ralph M. Riggs, *The Spirit Himself* (Springfield, Mo.: Gospel Publishing House, 1949), 53.

Chapter 1 Hot Coals from Heaven's Altar

1. Andrew Murray, *The Deeper Christian Life* (Shippensburg, Pa.: Destiny Image Classics, 2007), 126–7.

2. Evan Roberts' Testimony, revival-library.org.

3. A. B. Simpson, *The Supernatural* (Camp Hill, Pa.: Christian Publications, n.d.), 99.

4. R. A. Torrey, *The Person & Work of the Holy Spirit* (Grand Rapids: Zondervan, 1974), 61.

5. Murray, 75.

6. William Seymour, "In the Last Days," *The Apostolic Faith*, vol. 1, no. 9 (June-September 1907).

7. Francis MacNutt, Christian Healing Ministries, Inc., vol. 5, issue 5, 1.

Chapter 2 The Fire of Supernatural Anointing

1. Simpson, 99.

Chapter 3 The Fire of Boldness

1. "David Brainerd," compiled by Stephen Ross, wholesomewords.org.

2. R. A. Torrey, *How to Obtain Fullness of Power* (Springdale, Pa.: Whitaker House, 1982), 66.

3. Leonard Ravenhill, *Why Revival Tarries* (Minneapolis: Bethany House, 1959).

4. Charles Spurgeon, *Lectures to My Students* (Grand Rapids: Zondervan, 1954), 337.

Chapter 4 The Fire of Purity

1. Charles Spurgeon, *Let It Begin with Me: Spurgeon on Revival* (Ann Arbor, Mich.: Servant Publications, 1996), 81.
2. "Words of Repentance from Ted Haggard," July 7, 2009, charismamag.com.
3. Adrienne S. Gaines, "Earl Paulk's Former Church Sold," Charisma News Online, August 11, 2009, www.charismamag.com.
4. "Bishop Weeks Cussin' in the Bedroom," youtube.com. From a video message titled "The Mystery of Love" given at Global Destiny Church, Duluth, Georgia.

Chapter 5 The Fire of Integrity

1. Spurgeon, *Lectures to My Students*, 21.
2. Mike Guglielmucci, "Healer," Hillsong Music.
3. "Chart-topping Pastor's Cancer Lie," *Today Tonight*, reported by Sharon Smith, August 29, 2008, www.au.todaytonight.yahoo.com.
4. Larry Stockstill, *The Remnant* (Lake Mary, Fla.: Charisma House, 2008), iv.
5. "Gizelle Bryant vs. Jamal H. Bryant: Popular pastor and wife in divorce drama," *Path Magazine*, February 7, 2008, www.pathmagazine.com.

Chapter 6 The Fire of Humility

1. Eddie Hyatt, ed., *Fire on the Earth: Eyewitness Reports of the Azuza Street Revival* (Lake Mary, Fla.: Creation House Books, 2006), 67.
2. Spurgeon, *Lectures to My Students*, 201.
3. Jamie Buckingham, "God Is Shaking His Church," *Charisma*, June 1987, 21.
4. Leviathan is also mentioned in Psalm 74:14, Psalm 104:26 and Isaiah 27:1. Although some scholars have suggested that this animal was a crocodile, hippopotamus or whale, many creation scientists believe it was an aquatic dinosaur. Leviathan is often translated "sea monster."

Chapter 7 The Fire of Truth

1. Spurgeon, *Lectures to My Students*, 71.
2. David Wilkerson, audio message, "Reproach of the Solemn Assembly," http://www.intotruth.org/dev/reproach.htm.
3. "Todd Bentley / Lakeland, Florida / Anointed to Kick the Poor," www.youtube.com.
4. There are actually four types of cessationists: (1) Full cessationists believe all miracles have ceased today; (2) Classical cessationists believe that most miracles ceased after the New Testament was written, but that God occasionally works in supernatural ways today; (3) Consistent cessationists insist that, as miracles ceased after the early apostles, the need for New Testament apostles and prophets also ceased; and (4) Concentric cessationists teach that God still does miracles today, but only in unevangelized areas of the world.
5. Reports of heretical activity in Chinese underground churches were collected by the author during a trip to Hong Kong and Guangzhou, China, in January 2001.

Chapter 8 The Fire of Justice

1. Catherine Booth, *The Highway of Our God*, chapter 6, "Formalism or Grace," www.thegospeltruth.net/booth.
2. Thomas Hughes, *David Livingstone* (London: MacMillan & Company, 1906), 51.
3. David Wilkerson, audio message, "Reproach of the Solemn Assembly." http://www.intotruth.org/dev/reproach.htm.
4. Jim Bakker, letter dated June 20, 1992, mailed by Tammy Sue Chapman, New Covenant Church, Largo, Florida.
5. Kenneth Hagin Sr., *The Midas Touch* (Tulsa, Okla.: Kenneth Hagin Ministries, 2002).

Chapter 9 The Fire of Spiritual Liberty

1. "Mumford's Formal Repentance Statement to the Body of Christ," *Ministries Today*, January/February 1990, 52.
2. Ibid.
3. Ibid, 55.

Chapter 10 The Fire of Prayer

1. R. A. Torrey, *How to Obtain Fullness of Power* (Springdale, Pa.: Whitaker House, 1982), 71.
2. Mary Slessor, from "Missionary Quotes" compiled by Stephen Ross, www.wholesomewords.org/missions/msquotes.html.
3. E. M. Bounds, *Power through Prayer* (Chicago: Moody Classics, 2004), 52.
4. Dwight McKissic, "Statement Regarding August 29 Chapel," *New Blog for a Pneuma Time*, www.dwightmckissic.wordpress.com/2006/10/.
5. Ibid.
6. Kimberly Winston, "Speaking in Tongues: Faith's Language Barrier?" *USA Today*, May 24, 2007.
7. Jack Hayford, quoted by Steven Lawson in "The Foursquare Church Faces the 21st Century," *Charisma*, March 1993, 26.
8. Dennis and Rita Bennett, *The Holy Spirit and You* (Plainsfield, N.J.: Logos, 1971), 77.

Chapter 11 The Fire of Genuine Love

1. Hyatt, 78.

Chapter 12 How to Have Your Own Personal Pentecost

1. Corrie ten Boom, from *Good Reads Quotes*, www.goodreads.com/author/quotes/102203.Corrie_Ten_Boom.
2. Murray, 134.

Index

9/11, 77–78

Abihu, 85–86
Abram, 39–40
abstinence, 93
accessibility, 119
accountability, 66–67, 174
Ajo, Joel, 21
Ananias, 46
angels, 140–43
apostles
  abuse of title, 73–74, 172, 173
  as an essential ministry, 102–3
atonement. See salvation
authoritarianism, warning signs of
  lack of acceptance, 174–75
  lack of accountability, 174
  leadership characteristics, 175–76,
    177–78
  views of women, 178–79
Azusa Street Revival (1906–1909), 41,
  112

Bakker, Jim, 122, 155–56
Bakker, Tammy Faye, 122
Balaam, 67
baptism, 215

baptism in the Spirit, 40–41, 71–74, 224.
  See also fire of the Spirit; fresh bap-
  tism in the Spirit, preparation for;
  Pentecost, in the New Testament;
  wind of the Spirit
Basham, Don, 192
Bennett, Dennis, 192
Bennett, Rita, 192
Bentley, Todd, 64–65, 90, 91, 134–38
Bickle, Mike, 62, 96
Blackaby, Henry, 30
Blagojevich, Rod, 105
Booth, Catherine, 148, 212
Bounds, E. M., 180, 212
Brainerd, David, 68
Brother Andrew, 69, 212
Buckingham, Jamie, 122
Bynum, Juanita, 89

Cain, Paul, 59–62, 95–96
Campus Crusade for Christ, 128
Capps, Charles, 157
Cashwell, Gaston B., 213
Castro, Fidel, 19
celebrity preachers, 115–18, 126
cessationists, 228n4
Chambers, Oswald, 212

231

character, importance of, 63–64
charismatic movement
  as dead, 26, 28, 30
  historical overview of, 29
  new-generation churches of, 26–28
charlatans, danger signals of
  money-centered message, 162–63
  shepherds who do not feed their sheep,
    160–62
  taking the Lord's name in vain,
    163–65
China, house church movement in,
    54–55, 140
church leaders, forgiveness and restora-
    tion, 96–97
confession of sins, 94, 218
consecration, 215
conversion, 41
Copeland, Kenneth, 157
Cuba, charismatic movement in, 17–21

David, 211
Deere, Jack, 62, 96
deification of preachers, 63
discernment, 65–66, 132–34, 136, 139
discipleship models, 120
Discipleship Movement, 29, 169–71,
    178
Dobson, James, 192
Dollar, Creflo, 157
dunamis, 40, 190
DuPlantis, Jesse, 157
Duquesne revival (1967), 29

Edwards, Jonathan, 46
Eli, 106–7
Elijah, 40, 43
Elisha, 40, 55
Elymas (Bar-Jesus), 58
eternal punishment, 78, 85
evangelism, 28, 72–74, 76
  Jonah's experience in Nineveh, 207–9
evangelists, 103
Ezekiel
  rebuke of spiritual leaders, 134, 161
  vision of the river of God, 195–96

Finney, Charles G., 46, 212
fire of the Spirit, 32, 44–45
  counterfeit expressions of, 46–48
  in the hearts of post-Pentecost believ-
    ers, 211–12
  Old Testament encounters with,
    39–40, 211
  See also Pentecost, in the New
    Testament
fornication, 92–93
fresh baptism in the Spirit, preparation
  for, 215–17, 224–25
fruit of the Spirit, 64, 146–47

Gideon, 40
Giglio, Louie, 30
Gnosticism, 145
God, fear of, 94–95, 104
God's Smuggler (Brother Andrew), 69
Gomes, Harry, 51–53
Gonzalez, Emilio, 17, 19
Gospel, basics of, 78–79
Grady, J. Lee
  international ministries of, 113–15,
    199–201, 202–4
  overcoming an unwilling spirit, 218–20
  speaking in tongues, 181–84, 190
Graham, Billy, 73, 192–93
greed, 105, 155–57
grieving the Spirit, 217
Guglielmucci, Michael, 99–100

Haggard, Gayle, 82
Haggard, Ted, 81–83, 101
Hagin, Kenneth, Sr., 157
Harrison-Bryant, Jamal, 108–9
Hayford, Jack, 170, 191
"Healer" (Guglielmucci), 99
Hernandez, Rinaldo, 18, 19, 20, 21
Hinn, Benny, 156–57
Holiness Movement, 41
holiness revivals, 213
Holy Spirit and You, The (Bennett and
  Bennett), 192
Hophni, 106–7
Houston, Brian, 100
Howell, Richard, 53

Huldah, 211
humility, 123, 126–27, 174–75
    of Jesus, 115, 119, 127, 128
    of Paul, 117, 118–19
    See also leadership, principles for a
        humble ministry style
Hunter, Frances, 192
Hybels, Bill, 30

imposters, protection against, 63–67
Isaiah, 36, 40, 219

Jeet, 70
Jeremiah, 24, 211, 220
Jesus
    accessibility of, 119
    God's love revealed in, 79
    humility of, 115, 119, 127, 128
    ministry to Gentiles, 202, 205
    and the money-changers in the Tem-
        ple, 211
    primary mission of, 72
Jesus Movement, 73, 169
Jethro, 103–4
Jeyasingh, 70–71
John the Baptist, 43–44
John, the beloved disciple, 46
John, Sujo, 77
Jonah, 206–9
Jones, Jim, 173
Joshua, T. B., 131–32
Joyner, Rick, 62, 90, 96

Kelechi, 69–70
Korah, 67
Koresh, David, 173
Kuhlman, Kathryn, 46

Lakeland Revival, 64–65, 90, 134–38
leadership,
    biblical guidelines for, 63–64, 109,
        168–70, 176
    God's requirements for, 104–5
    principles for a humble ministry style,
        119–20
    rules for, 109–11
Leap of Faith (1992), 154–55

Lee, Lewis, 74–77
Leverette, June, 182–83
Livingstone, David, 148

MacNutt, Francis, 45
Manepally, Laxmi, 52
Manepally, Mesheck, 52
Manepally, Varaprasad, 52
Maranatha Campus Ministries, 171–72
Mason, C. H., 213
McKissic, Dwight, 185
McManus, Erwin, 30
men, types of relationships between
    "Barnabases," 119–20
    "Pauls," 119
    "Timothys," 120
Midas Touch, The (Hagin), 157–59
ministers, common dysfunctions
    among, 102
miracles
    discernment, 56–59
    in non-Western cultures, 51–55
    and Western-style intellectualism,
        55–56
Moody, D. L., 41
Moore, Beth, 30
Moses, 56
Mumford, Bob, 166, 171
Murray, Andrew, 36, 41, 210, 212
mutual cooperation, 128

Nadab, 85–86
Nebuchadnezzar, 123
Nee, Watchman, 212
Newberg, Andrew B., 188

ordination, 137
Otoniel ("Pastor Oto"), 70

pastors, 103
Patterson, Paige, 185
Paul, 46, 63
    attitude toward immorality, 90–91
    cautions regarding spiritual gifts,
        139–40
    experience of speaking in tongues,
        183, 187–88

humility of, 117, 118–19
and Pentecost, 43
qualifications for leaders, 63–64, 109, 176
treatment of wayward leaders, 107–8, 110–11
Paulk, Donnie Earl, 84
Paulk, Earl, 83–84, 93
Pensacola Revival (1995), 29
Pentecost
in the New Testament, 31–32, 43
observance of by Christians, 42–43
Old Covenant version of, 43
Pentecostal revivals, 41–42, 213
Phinehas, 106–7
porneia, 92
Pothabathula, Jyothi, 51–52
Pothabathula, Nagamani, 51–52
Pothabathula, Suribabu, 51
praying in the Spirit. *See* speaking in tongues (*glossolalia*)
praying in tongues. *See* speaking in tongues (*glossolalia*)
pride, 64, 103
Leviathan as representation of, 125
manifestations of, 125–28
as the motivation of false prophets, 145
and the quenching of the Spirit, 217
as spiritual abuse, 121–24
prophets, 103
abuse, 73–74
false prophets, 145
true prophets, 144
prosperity gospel, the, 152–54, 155–60, 162

quenching the Spirit, 217–20

racism, destruction of, 27–28, 201–4, 205–6
Ravenhill, Leonard, 68
redemption. *See* salvation
regeneration, 41
Remnant, The (Stockstill), 101–2
repentance, 91, 94
Roberts, Evan, 37–39
four-point plan, 39
Robertson, Pat, 170

salvation, 79, 224
Samson, 101, 103
sanctification, 41, 42
Sapphira, 46
Satan, 121, 163, 187, 204
Savelle, Jerry, 157
second baptism. *See* baptism in the Spirit
second blessing. *See* baptism in the Spirit
self-denial. *See* humility
self-discipline, 93–94
sensationalism, 64–65
Serrano, Jorge, 167–68
servanthood, 125–26
sexual sin, steps for dealing with, 92–95
Seymour, William J., 41–42, 198, 212, 213
Shepherding Movement. *See* Discipleship Movement
Simon the magician, 65
Simpson, A. B., 41, 50, 212
sin, 78, 106–8
"slain in the Spirit," 45–47
counterfeit expressions of, 46–48, 64
Slessor, Mary, 180
Slumdog Millionaire (2008), 149–50
Solomon, 103
Solomon, Raja J., 201
speaking in tongues (*glossolalia*), 183–87, 224
and going deeper with God, 194–97
Grady's experience of, 181–84, 190
"initial evidence" teaching about, 191
Paul's experience of, 196
reasons for, 187–90
spiritual gifts (*charismata*), 132, 138–40
New Testament principles of, 144–47
See also discernment; speaking in tongues (*glossolalia*)
Spurgeon, Charles, 24, 78, 80, 98, 112, 130, 212
St. Clair, Barry, 120
Stanley, Andy, 30
Stockstill, Larry, 100–103, 108

teachers, 103
televangelism scandals (1987), 29
ten Boom, Corrie, 210, 212
testing the spirits. *See* discernment
Thampy, Biju, 149–51
Toronto Blessing (1994), 29
Torrey, R. A., 41, 68, 180
truth telling, 104–5

Warren, Rick, 30
Weeks, Thomas Wesley, III, 86, 89
Weiner, Bob, 171
Welsh revival (1904), 38, 39
Wesley, John, 40–41, 46, 212

White, Paula, 88–89
White, Randy, 88
Whitefield, George, 212
Wilkerson, David, 130, 148
wind of the Spirit, 31–33, 44
Winfrey, Oprah, 133
Woodworth-Etter, Maria, 46

Xuan, 71

Youth With A Mission, 128

zeo, 212

J. Lee Grady has been involved in Christian journalism since he graduated from Berry College in Rome, Georgia, in 1979. After serving eight years as editor of *The Forerunner*, an evangelistic newspaper aimed at college students, and after editing *National and International Religion Report* in Washington, D.C., for three years, he began a lengthy career at *Charisma* magazine in Orlando, Florida. He served there for seventeen years and won numerous awards for his reporting. In 1996 he was honored by *Christianity Today* as one of forty emerging American evangelical leaders under age forty.

While at *Charisma*, he also became known for his regular "Fire in My Bones" column, in which he challenged the church to return to integrity, holiness and authentic faith. He continues to write that column today (www.fireinmybones.com) while serving as editor of *Experience*, an online magazine published by the International Pentecostal Holiness Church. Lee was ordained by that denomination in 2000.

That same year, Lee began to shift his work more aggressively toward the preaching ministry. After publishing *10 Lies the Church Tells Women* and *25 Tough Questions About Women and the Church* (both from Charisma House), he founded The Mordecai Project, an effort aimed at empowering women leaders and confronting the abuse of women around the world. He has now taken his message of liberation to more than 24 countries, and has addressed conferences in Africa, Asia, Latin America, Europe, North America and Australia. He also confronts men about the abuse of women in their cultures. His next book, *10 Lies Men Believe*, will be published in 2010 by Charisma House.

Lee and his wife, Deborah, have four grown daughters. When he's not writing or traveling, he enjoys coffee, crossword puzzles, jogging, theme parks, classic movies, ethnic food and listening to crickets and thunderstorms from his back porch.

To learn more about his ministry, go to:
www.themordecaiproject.com
Or write:
Lee Grady
Experience Magazine
P.O. Box 9
Franklin Springs, GA 30639

More Insight into the Pentecostal and Charismatic Churches

"This is a must-read history."
—Francis MacNutt, Ph.D., co-founder, Christian Healing Ministries

Premier Pentecostal historian Vinson Synan—widely respected for his scholarship and balance—holds a unique position: personal involvement in many of the extraordinary events of the last hundred years. Events that gave birth to the charismatic and Pentecostal movements.

Now, for the first time, he candidly shares exciting behind-the-scenes stories and personal assessments of these phenomenal experiences, including:

- when the Holy Spirit fell at Azusa Street,
- the surprising birth of the charismatic renewal,
- the Latter Rain movement,
- the emergence of charismatic Catholicism,
- the Toronto Blessing
- and more!

An Eyewitness Remembers the Century of the Holy Spirit
by Vinson Synan

Chosen
a division of Baker Publishing Group
www.chosenbooks.com

Revolutionize Your Prayer Life

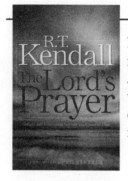

No prayer is better known—or more misunderstood—than the Lord's Prayer, the prayer Jesus provided in his Sermon on the Mount. With wisdom and depth, Dr. R. T. Kendall turns a keen eye to this amazing prayer, unlocking life-changing revelations contained in each line, including:

- interpreting and praying in the will of God,
- the purpose of the Lord's Prayer,
- how unanswered prayer can be a sign of God's favor,
- why you should pray at all
- and more.

Not only will you discover a new model for prayer, but you will also find insight and inspiration to draw you closer to the Father.

The Lord's Prayer by Dr. R. T. Kendall

a division of Baker Publishing Group

www.chosenbooks.com